THE
TOMHORN LEGGHORN
COMPLETE
HILLBILLY DIKSHUNERY

Tomhorn Legghorn
AKA
Thomas C. Legg

ILLUTRATED by Terry Lake

Thomas C. Legg
Publisher

Coldwater, Michigan, USA

Thomas C. Legg, Publisher
61 East Chicago Street
Coldwater, Michigan 49036

Book design by Thomas C. Legg and
Terry Lake

Library of Congress in-Publication Data
Tomhorn Legghorn
Hillbilly Dikshunery, The Tomhorn
Legghorn Complete / Thomas C. Legg---
1st ed.

ISBN: 0-9672121-0-3
Library of Congress Card Number:
00-190678

FIRST PAPERBACK EDITION

FORWARD

Let me start right out by telling you that
this is not a *Southern, Appalachian, Ozark
or Texarkana* dictionary, nor is it limited to
any region of the country. While I recognize
that it is in these areas of the country that
hillbillies and their language originated, the
modern reality is that in the highly mobile
American society, one will find what I refer
to as *Hillbillies*, throughout North America.
Therefore we shall first define what
Hillbilly means, within the context of this
book, then just a brief word on the origins
of most of the language usage and phonetics
that are the subject of this work and the
purpose and intended use of this volume by
you, the student of cultural diversity.

While once the term *Hillbilly* meant the
simple hard working and deeply religious
Protestant white folks, who settled first in
the Appalachians and later in the Ozarks and

West, the term has over the last 20-30 years come to mean uneducated, unsophisticated white people who are often unemployed or unskilled laborers and have variously also been referred to as *Rednecks, Bumpkins* and *Trailer Park Trash*. These people can be found throughout the United States and even in Canada, however, for all their shortcomings, the Canadians do have an excellent educational system that discourages such ignorance. Of course the US educational system is largely responsible for the growth of hillbilly speech, since its more concerned with teaching self esteem, cultural diversity, condom use, environmentalism and "just say no" than it is in wasting a bunch of time on trivialities like "reedin an' rytin", but I digress. Hillbillies can now be found in virtually every state, in rural and urban areas, but are most concentrated in the industrial areas where they gravitated towards the industrial jobs from the late 30s to mid 60s.

The Tomhorn Legghorn Complete Hillbilly Dikshunery

Let me be clear that I mean no offense to anybody in writing this book. It is chock full O' stereotypes, clichés and broad generalizations, for which I make no apologies, but I think as you read it you will see things that you recognize as true and that is the humor and irony of this work, as in most of life. If you are extremely politically correct and have no sense of humor or are easily offended by laughing at yourself or others, then this might not be a good read for you. If, on the other hand, you have a keen enough sense of humor to recognize the comic elements in modern American society, maybe even in yourself and those around you, then I believe that you will find this work quite funny, as well as informative. I, myself, have been known to use some of the words and phrases contained herein, both in jest and in all seriousness and, yes, some of my best friends are hillbillies (I warned you about the clichés). In any event, I'm not intending

iii

to put anyone down here, however, it certainly would appear that way and in places that is certainly the result, but that is sometimes the nature of pointing out the humor in society and situations.

The origins of hillbilly speech really go back to the earliest of English and Scottish settlers in New England and the Mid-Atlantic regions. The lower classes of urban England and the Northern Highlands brought with them many of their phonetic variations of the "King's English". Some examples are; ain't, twernt, twas, nairy and a host of others. These usages were liberally added to by not only other Europeans and their particular corruption of the English language, but were further colored with the English adopted by the African Slaves that were brought to North America.

While the primary intent of this book is humor and light entertainment, the author also believes, or at least hopes, that it has

some educational value for students of
American English and its dialects and
corruption. I believe that this is a fairly
complete study of most of the commonly
used pronunciations and usages among the
hillbilly people. This is, however, merely a
first edition and I'm sure that I missed
numerous words, phrases and usages, some
obscure and probably even some that I will
be highly embarrassed to find that I missed.
In fact I kept thinking of so many new ones
as this work progressed over a painful 3
years, that I am already aware of some that
were omitted. The simple fact of the matter
is, however, that this book took about a year
and a half longer than anticipated due to new
entries occurring to me or otherwise coming
to my attention as work and edits
progressed. I finally got to the point where I
simply threw up my hands and hollered
"SCREW IT!" and decided that I could add
these to later editions along with those that
I'm sure will come flowing in from the

millions of readers who will enjoy this book, but nearly as much as they will enjoy pointing out my shortcomings and downright ignorance for forgetting some obvious gems of the hillbilly language. With this in mind, feel free to send me any suggestions you have to the address of the publisher as listed in the prelude to this book or via email to my email address as listed herein or by visiting my website.

Thank you for buying this book and allowing me to defray some of the expense of publishing it. I truly hope you enjoy it, but if not, don't bitch to me about it.

Tomhorn Legghorn
Coldwater, Michigan
Email: tomhorn5@worldnet.att.net

HILLBILLY HUNTN

ACKNOWLEDGEMENTS

The Author would like to gratefully thank and acknowledge the following people for their invaluable help in producing this work, but try not to blame them.

Foremost I wish to thank Steve "More Beer" Whitcomb, who came up with the original idea for this book, but who wisely gave up on following through with it. Thanks to my significant other Kristin Corlett for putting up with me generally and during the work on this book and for urging me to get the damn thing done. I would like to thank my parents Louis Legg Jr. and Joan Legg for their encouragement and patience with me and thanks to my Brother Louis III for his professional advice as a writer. Also thanks to my sister in law Shanon and her's and Louis III's children Matthew and Jonathon for actually finding this stuff entertaining. Thanks also to Carl Clatterbuck for his professional assistance.

I would also like to gratefully acknowledge all of those who encouraged this work and contributed ideas and suggestions, particularly the following: Steve "Guido" Trylick, Trent Chambers, Steve "Crusty" Rotenberg, Edwin Paquette, Tim "Officer Friendly" Haukswell, Joe Romano, Greg "Griz" Flynn, LaTisha and Aaron Tuhacek, Galen, Hillary, Alison and Judith Corlett, Steve Bommer, Ralph Moore, Karl Heath, Bill "Wild Willy" Ellis, Vern MacMahan Wayne Moyer, Gary Hiesler, Benny Parsons, Dr. Jerry Punch, Buddy Baker, Ned Jarret, the Earnhardts, the Pettys and the Burton Brothers.

Finally I wish to acknowledge my ex-wife Sharon and her entire family for contributing to this book, just by speaking and especially her brother, Mike Fry, who speaks fluent hillbilly and is one of the kindest, yet roughest, people that I have ever met. I miss him, which is more than I can say for my ex-wife.

A

ACROST *prep.* Across. A common hillbilly usage, in which they add an "ed" to the end, but then, as hillbillies are inclined to, they replace the "ed" at the end of a word with a "t" sound. As in: "he retcht rot acrost n grapt me."

AFFORE *adv.* Before. In front of or ahead in time or space. This is a widely used hillbillyism, as in: "Doan caste yer pearls affore swine."

AGGIN *adv.* Again. As in: "not aggin." Also, *prep.* Against. As in: "hiffn ya ain't fer us, yer aggin us." Used fairly widely as *again*, but most commonly in the

Southeast and Mid Atlantic as *against*.

AH *pron.* I. Does this really need an explanation? Widely used throughout the country.

AHAINNA *contraction* of I am not, which is of course actually a contraction of the grammatical nightmare; I ain't. As in: "Ahainna goin." Widely used throughout the country.

AHDA *contraction* of I and would or I would have. I'd or I'd have. Widely used, this is an expression of intention, as in: "Ahda be wawtchin ma mouth fizu baw."

AHIND *adv.* Behind. To or towards the rear, in back of or late. This one is widely used, as in: "Git thee ahind me Satan."

2

AHMA *contraction* of I and am. The first person expression of intent. Used by the lazy-spoken everywhere. This probably has roots as much in the speech patterns that developed among the Africans that were brought as slaves to the old South as in any European dialect, but has become amalgamated into non-ethnic American usage. This pronunciation is still mostly indigenous to the South and is often followed by the word: "gawna."

AHZA *contraction* of I am. "Ahza fixin' ta go uptown." This is a pronunciation that probably comes from Old South Black colloquial, not much heard anymore, but once a standard Southern hillbilly expression. It is probably seeing

3

less legitimate use, because it is one of those words that have become cliché.

AIGS *n.* Eggs. A breakfast favorite with "baikin n grits" in the South or with "haish bronze" in the North. Widely used throughout the country, except the West Coast, Northeast and far North, where they actually say "hash Browns."

AIN'T *contraction* of is and not. Is not or are not or am not. This is, of course, an old hillbilly standard. Widely used throughout the country. In some regions of the country, particularly the Upper Mississippi and Ohio Valleys and the Great Lakes, when used after words ending with vowel sounds, this word often will begin with the letter H. See also **HAIN'T**.

4

AKSHULL *adj.* Actual. Factual or real. This is the preferred pronunciation of this word by hillbillies everywhere. **AKSULLY** *adv.*

AMBLIENSE *n.* Ambulance. For hillbillies any minor emergency is cause for summoning an "ambliense", since the hillbilly will certainly never pay for it. Widely used throughout the country.

AMOAN *contraction* of I am going. A further contraction is **AMOANNA**, for I am going to. This expression is mostly heard in the South from Texas through the Piedmont.

AN *conj.* Together with along with or connected to. Also used to join together words. This enjoys very wide usage, as in: "Its jus him an me."

ARE *n*. Air. This one is a fairly hard core Deep South pronunciation, which is not heard much anymore, except in the Southern Appalachian region.

ARGY *v*. Argue. Also known as "*carryin awn.*" Another relic of the old Deep South.

ARN *n*. Iron. This is mostly Southern and Western as in: "Thet Thar rail iz made outta arn." Also *v*. To iron. -*pres. tense* **ARNIN** Ironing. An example of usage is: "Maw tuck in sum arnin fer extry money."

ASKEERT *past tense* of *v*. to scare. Scared. As in: "Ah hain't askeert a yew." Hard core trailer park pronunciation, particularly

6

popular in the Midwest, Ohio Valley and Great Lakes. See also **SKEERT.**

ASPOSTA *contraction of,* supposed to. As in: "Ya hain't asposta do that." Used sparsely throughout the country, mostly by illiterates. See also **POSTA.**

AST *past tense.* of *v.* to ask. Asked. Used fairly widely throughout North America.

ATNAIR *contraction* of that one there. A reference to a specific item, this word can even be expanded further to **ATNAIRZA,** as in: "Atnairza owneyus wun;" or **ATNAIRILL,** as in: "Atnairill work." This word is a prime example of how efficiently hillbillies can save considerable verbage by condensing three

words into two syllables. Most
common in the Appalacians and
Piedmont of the Southeast.

ATSA *contraction* of that is a.
"Atsa mot purtee sot." Very
widely used everywhere

ATTAIR *contraction* of that there.
When Lee Bob has completed a
job to his satisfaction he might
say: "Attair is a huntin' dawg,"
indicating that it will work well,
like a well trained hound.
Particularly popular in the
Southeast and Mississippi and
Ohio Valleys.

AWL *n.* Oil. This is primarily a
Southern pronunciation, but is
heard fairly commonly elsewhere.
It can mean any kind of oil, but
usually is used in reference to
motor oil.

AWN *prep.* On. Indicating position or placement, as in: "Its awn the table." Also many other usages, such as to indicate an occurrence, state condition or process, as in: "on far," "on bidness," or "on the phone," just to name a few. This usage has its origins in the South, but is now widely used.

AWROT *adv.* All right or its common misspelling, alright. This is very widely heard among hillbillies everywhere and even among non-hillbillies in the South, as in: "Well awrot."

AYETALIEN *adj.* Italian. This one has become almost cliché, but is still legitimately heard among older folks in the Southeast and Deep South. To say this properly, there must be strong emphasis on the first syllable.

AYUS *n.* Ass. The classic example is: "Kiss mah ayus." A pronunciation that is used widely when the speaker wants to emphasize the word ass.

AXSESSORIES *n. plur.* Accessories. Heard appallingly often, especially in the North and West.

B

BADDER *adj*. Meaner or tougher. This is heard widely among the lower elements of North American society, as in: "Doan be messin with me, cause Ahma badder n yew."

BAICK *n*. Back. Not the front, but on or in the other side. This is pretty much exclusively the Southern pronunciation, as in: "Yawl come baick now, ya hear?"

BAIG *n*. Bag. Also *v*. to bag, as in to catch or kill while hunting. – *past tense* **BAIGED**. A Central River Valleys and Southeastern Piedmont classic. "Ah baiged me a buck."

BAIKIN *n*. Bacon. This is the Northern and Western version of

11

this pork product, ususally eaten
for breakfast with "aigs." See also
BIKIN for the Southern
pronunciation

BALD *past tense* of *v.* to boil.
Boiled. This is the Southeastern
and Deep South version. See also
BILED.

BAMA *n.* Alabama. Actually they
don't say it that way in Alabama
much, unless referring to the
University of Alabama, but
hillbillies throughout much of the
rest of the continent, especially
Yankee trailer park types, just
love to refer to the whole state in
this manner

BAR *n.* Bear. For you city folks,
these things are not cute, cuddly
playful little things, but are, in
fact big, ugly, vile smelling,

surprisingly strong and fast mounds of matted fur, with huge, razor sharp teeth and claws, that eat household garbage and pets, but only after rolling in them. Ol' Jeb might be heard to say: "Ah seen me attair bar a comin' outta ta henhouse aggin." This is a predominantly Southern and Western pronunciation. It should also be noted that in Alabama, this refers to the much revered "Bear" Bryant, the late football coach for the University of Alabama, known in that state as "Bama."

BARREE *v.* To borrow. This is used in all hillbilly regions to mean the loan of an item, with or without permission. **BARD** *past tense* As in: "Ah bard paws core without axin im."

13

BAW *n.* Boy. This is usually an insult, unless addressed towards ones own son, in which case it's the only thing that "yer Paw" ever calls you, besides "Git wood" and "Shut up", if you're a hillbilly. Used widely, but the farther North you get the more it starts to actually sound like "boy". Nonetheless, Northern hillbillies say this when belittling a man or addressing their son(s).

BELLERIN *pres.* tense of *v.* to yell. Yelling, crying, whining or generally "careynon." Widely used.

BERTHIN *v.* to give birth to. A common usage, especially in the South, as in: "Betty Sue's berthin another yungun."

BERTHT *past participle*. Born. Mostly Southern.

BESTEST *adj*. Best. Even though in true English *best* means of the highest quality, the most desirable, superior or the greatest, this doesn't seem to satisfy the hillbilly mind. They apparently believe that more emphasis is required so to hillbillies the finest of things aren't just "the best", but they are "the bestest."

BETTERN *contraction of* better than. This one enjoys wide usage, as in: "M folks is hoytitoyti an thanks theyz bettern usnz."

BIDNISS *n*. Business. Commercial activities or trade. Ones occupation. Commercial, trade or industrial establishment. All hillbillies have an aspiration to be in "bidniss fer theysefs," since, as all hillbillies know, being in any business makes one an instant millionaire. This is the primarily Northern and Western pronunciation. Also can mean to concern oneself with, as in: "Tain't nun O yer bidniss." See also **BINNISS** for the Southern and Eastern usage.

BIDNISSMAN *n.* Businessman. A man who is in business for himself or owns a commercial or industrial enterprise. This is the pronunciation in Northern and Western regions. See also **BINNISSMAIN** for the Southern usage.

BIKIN *n.* Bacon. As in: "Ahmoan have me sum bikin n' aigs." This

is the Southern pronunciation. See
BAIKIN for the Northern version.

BILED *past tense* of *v.* to boil.
Boiled. This is the Western and
Northern version. See also **BALD**

BILLY BADASS *n.* Generic term
among hillbillies to denote
someone in a state in which they
fancy themselves invincible or are
challenging others to "fottin' er
feudin'." You will find this quaint
little label anywhere you find
hard-core trailer trash.

BIN *past tense* of *v.* to be. Been. As
in: "Bin thar, dunn that." Used
widely, except near the Canadian
Border, where they say: "bean."

BINNISS *n.* Business. This is the
primarily Southern and Eastern
pronunciation. See also **BIDNISS**

BILLY BADASS

for the Northern and Western usage.

BINNISSMAIN *n.* Businessman. The Southern pronunciation. See also **BIDNISSMAN** for the Northern and Western usage.

BISKITS *n.* Biscuits. A southern usage and primarily a Southern food, served with nearly every meal, whether for breakfast, with "sawsitch n' grivey", or for dinner or supper, with anything.

BITCH SLAP *v.* to strike suddenly to the side of the head or generally "thump" ones head. Often used as a threat, as in: "Bwa, doan be messin' with me er Ah'll bitch slap yer ayus." Heard anywhere that Billy Badass is found and usually uttered by the one currently fancying himself as such.

BLOWED –*past tense* of *v*. to blow. Blown. While originating in the South, this one is now heard everywhere. This word is often paired with up, to form the famous expression: "Blowed up." An example is: "Ah wuz jes drivin' along an the motor blowed up."

BOADASHUS *adj.* Powerful, intense or grand. Can have positive connotations, as in; "Thet was one boadashus rasslin' match," but can also be bad, as in; "Ah gots me one boadashus hankerin fer some vittels." Predominantly Southeastern and Deep Southern.

BOB WAAR *n.* Barbed Wire. This is a common fencing material, as in:

"Thet Jile's hard ta bust outta on accounta they got em thet bob waar fence."

BOMB FAR *n*. Bon fire. To do it right, a really massive pile of wood, soaked with gasoline is to be ignited by someone who has recently drunk about two cases of Bud. Widely used.

BORNED *past participle* of birth. This is the Northern pronunciation. See **BERTHT** for the Southern version.

BREECHES *n*. Pants, slacks, trousers or jeans of any description. This brings to mind a the story of a hillbilly I know who went to a Country Club to meet some city relations. When he arrived wearing blue jeans, with his shirt and wide tie and wide lapelled rayon suit, the Maitre'd informed him that jeans were not allowed and that arrangements could be made to provide suitable trousers from spares kept in the locker room. The hillbilly responded loudly: "Ah hain't eatin ma supper in somebody else's breeches, baw!" He ate his meal dressed as he was. A truly multi regional expression.

BRUNG *–past tenseI of* v. to bring. Brought. This word is heard very widely and way too often.

BUFFETTE *n.* Buffet restaurants are a cornerstone of hillbilly life everywhere. Special occasions like birthdays, anniversaries, NASCAR races or payday are all occasions "fer packin' up maw n' the youngunz an headin' on down

ta the Kountry Kitchen Buffette
fer all the vittles ya kin eat."

<u>C</u>

CACKULATE *v.* Calculate or think.
When a hillbilly has some sort of
proposal to make, they will
usually begin by saying; "Ta way
Ah cackulate it. . ." Used quite
widely, but more common in the
Northern and Western states,
because most Southerners and
Central River Valley hillbillies
prefer to use the word "reckon."

CAIN'T *contraction of can and not.*
Can't. This usage derives from the
South, but has infiltrated hillbilly
life everywhere. This one is heard
all the time.

CALIFORNY *n.* The state of
California. This pronunciation is
most common in the Mid South
and Arklatex regions.

24

CALVARY *pron.* Cavalry. A widely mispronounced word among hillbillies. They often confuse the mounted armed forces divisions with the hill on which Jesus Christ was crucified and vice versa.

CAREYNON *contraction of* carrying and on. Usually means arguing, or being boisterous, as in: "M 2 was careynon."

CATTERWALLIN' *pres* tense of *v.* to cry. Crying, whining and generally "careynon." Paw might tell the "yunguns" to "Stop thet damn catterwallin'."

CHIMBLY *n.* Chimney. This is a classic illustration of how a fairly simple word can be fumbled about in a manner that leaves the listener with the impression that the speaker has never seen the word in print or couldn't sound it out if they did. As in: "Ta Christmas tom, Sandyclause comes daywn the chimbly."

CHITLINS *n.* A food known in old England as Chitterlings. Actually this is a very disgusting food made from the intestines of a pig, or "hawg," which I would not eat on a dare. This is mostly a Southern word and food.

CITYSLICKER *n.* A person from any city with a population greater than 2,000. As in: 'M cityslickers awl thank theyz bettern usnz." A very popular usage among rural hillbillies everywhere.

COCOLA *prop. n.* Coca Cola. This is a strictly Southeastern and Deep South phoneticism. "Set on daywn n grap ya a Cocola." See also **SOADYPOP** for the Northcentral version

CORE *n.* Car. A deep South pronunciation. As one moves North it becomes "car" then eventually, if you go way North and East, it becomes "kaa."

COUNSEL *n.* Console. Hillbillies don't know the meaning of getting counsel. To them this word means the elbow rest and change tray between bucket seats in an automobile or large furniture like television set. Used widely and heard frighteningly often.

CRAISH *n.* Crash or *v.* To crash. This is primarily a Southern usage, which almost always indicates an automobile collision.

CORE

CRAFT *n.* Carafe. This dandy can be seen right in print on restaurant menus, mostly in the Midwestern states, Central River Valleys, Great Lakes and Plains, but has also been observed by the author in the South and West too. The establishments that use this are usually small town "swanky" joints, who fancy themselves as fine dining establishments, but they roll the tin flatware in paper napkins, tell you to keep your fork as they whisk away your salad plate and have waitresses, never waiters, who call you "Hun" in french maid outfits. And tonights special? "Well, hun, idbe prom reeyab, biked taiter n a craft a chablease." Of course the ch in chablis is pronounced as in Charlie.

CRICK *n.* Creek. "Yawl youngunz run awn daywn ta the crick n' fetch some wawter." This is a rural pronunciation that is especially popular in the Mid States and the West.

CRITTER *n.* Animal. This indicates any animal, insect or other ambulatory living being whatsoever. This originates from the South, but is heard fairly widely elsewhere and has become somewhat cliché.

CROM *n.* Crime. Mostly a Southern Pronunciation, this is used to denote either a criminal activity or something that the speaker considers unacceptable, as in: "The way thet feller treats M youngunz iz a crom."

CUMAWN *contraction* of come and on. Come on. Widely used, this is an invitation for others to accompany the speaker to go along with them, as in: "Cumawn, weez a goan uptaywn." It can also be a plea to be agreeable or allow something, as in: "Cumawn Maw, kin we go ta the rices?" This expression is also very often used alone as an invitation to fight. When this usage is invoked, the one inviting the fight will usually hold both hands extended straight out from elbows tucked closely to the sides of the torso, with palms up and fingers raised and moved back and forth in unison as this expression is growled menacingly.

CUSS *v.* To swear or use profanity. Used everywhere. An example might be a sibling stating: "Maw, Joe Bob used a cuss word."

CUZN *n.* also *conj.* This gem has two meanings: cousin, the noun; and because, the most specific conjunction in the English language to express causation or reason. The former is by far the more widely used, as in: "How ya doin cuzn." The more obscure usage, as in: "Ahma gonna do it cuzn ah wants ta." This later usage is only heard among the truly ignorant trailer park trash.

D

DAH *v.* To die. The act of life ending. Mostly a Southern pronunciation. **DODD** *past tense* Died. **DONN** *pres. tense* Dying.

DAID *adj.* Dead. Not alive, expired. This word originated in the south, but has spread elsewhere.

DAWG *n.* Dog. Hillbillies love their dogs. As in: "Clem likes his goodawl huntin' hound, wholst Crystal, she purfurs M little kick dawgs." This is pretty much a rural standard everywhere, especially in the South and West.

DAYWN *adv.* or *n.* Down. This must be pronounced in one syllable.

DAWG

This is strictly a Southern pronunciation.

DEATH *adj.* Deaf. This is an extremely common hillbilly misuse, as in: "It ain't gawna dew no good tawkin' ta thet baw, he's death."

DEETROIT *place.* Detroit, Michigan. This is not exactly a garden spot, but has a huge variety of people and all sorts of hillbillies. There are Lebanese rednecks and black NASCAR fans in the Greater Detroit area, thus proving that trailer park trash knows no racial or ethnic boundaries.

DEEVAN *n.* Sofa or couch. As in: "C'mon in, take a load off, have yerseff a flop daywn on the deevan." Used quite widely, but most popular in the Deep South, Central River Valleys and Mid States.

DEEVORSE *n*. or *v*. Divorce. This a hillbilly ritual that is so widely enjoyed that many hillbillies do it quite a few times, but never until they want to get married again. Billy Bob might say: "Me n Mary Lou cain't git hitcht til ma deevorse is fonnel." Mostly a Southern and Western pronunciation.

DEW *v*. Do. This is, strictly speaking, not just a hillbilly pronunciation, but the way that all English speaking people pronounce it, but hillbillies seem, somehow, to emphasize the "w" sound when using this word.

DIFFURNZ *n.* Difference. Dissimilar, diverse or a degree of variation. Unlike. This is heard far and wide, as in: "It doan maike no diffurnz nohow."

DIHUNT *contraction* of did and not. Didn't. Nine out of ten hillbillies who use this word prefer this pronunciation, as in: "Ah dihunt never date ma cuzn. Screwed er a few toms, but never tuck er out fust."

DILAPILATED *adj.* Dilapidated. In a state of disrepair or run down. A hillbilly might defend the state of his trailer by saying; "R haywz may look dilapilated, but its home." This is especially popular in the Midwestern states, Central River Valleys and Great Lakes, but is quite common everywhere as well.

DINCHA *contraction* of didn't and you. This is heard very commonly among a wide segment of society and is practically the standard North American pronounciation.

DOAN *contraction* of do and not. Literally translated as don't. Often used improperly in place of doesn't and almost always used as part of a double negative, as in; "It doan make no diffurnz nohow." You may note that strictly speaking, this is not grammatically correct, as it should be: "It *doesn't* make *any* difference." This brings up an important point in hillbilly word usage, not only in the penchant for the double negative, but also in the universal usage of the hillbilly variant of the contraction of *do* and not, in place of that for *does* and not.

DOANCHA *contraction* of don't and you. Of course this one has a contraction within a contraction, thus being an excellent example of hillbilly verbal economy. Heard virtually everywhere in North America. Also sometimes pronounced **DOANCHEW.**

DOM *n.* Dime. This is the way Southerners, in general, refer to the ten-cent coin.

DORLIN *n.* Darling. A uniquely Southern usage, as in: "Ma Dorlin, Ah luv ya."

DOT HIS (HER) EYE *true hillbilly expression.* To punch one in the eye, thus leaving a bruise. This is often used as a threat, as in; "Ah'll dot his eye, hiffn he doan

leave ma gal alone." A popular
favorite with hard core hillbillies,
wherever and whenever they can
be found angry.

DRAH *adj.* Dry. Mostly of Southern
origin, but a popular hillbilly
pronunciation elsewhere, as well.
"Fetch me a beer, cuzn maw
maywth shore is drah."

DRANKIN' *pres. tense* of *v.* to
drink. Drinking. Almost always,
this will be a reference to
consuming alcoholic beverages,
usually beer, whiskey or
moonshine. This is a serious
pursuit for hillbillies and they
indulge in it on a regular basis.
This one enjoys wide usage.

DROT *n.* Drought. An extremely dry
atmospheric condition which
persists over a considerable

period of time. This is mostly
heard in the South and West.

DUN *mod.* Done. This word is not
only used in the traditional
English language sense, but in
also injected before a verb in
nearly any situation, as in; "Ah
dun tolt ya wunst, ah hain't tellin
ya aggin." This usage enjoys
extensive, universal usage among
hillbillies.

DUNNER *mod.* More well done.
This is fairly common, especially
when expressing a preference for
the degree to which a piece of
meat is cooked. Sally Jean might
well demand: "Ah wants thissear
steak dunner." This is another
widely used term among
hillbillies.

41

E

EAZTROTH *n.* Eaves trough. A means of carrying rainwater along the eaves edge of a roof. A very widely used term.

ER *conj.* Or. Used to indicate alternatives, either singular or plural. As in: "its us er them." Very broadly and commonly used among many people, even by those who would not be considered as hard core hillbillies. Also *pron.* Her. Also a wide usage.

ESPLAIN *v.* Explain. To make understood or to clarify a fact or subject. This is a fairly common, but somewhat arcane, pronunciation among hillbillies far and wide. This usage is seen most commonly at the beginning of a statement or following words ending in consonant sounds, as in: "Esplain it." See also the more obscure and narrow usage, **SPLAIN.**

ESTATIC *adj.* Ecstatic. A state of excitement or rapture. This is one of my personal favorites, which I hear appallingly often among those of limited education and social graces.

ETLENNA *n.* Atlanta, Georgia. A big Southern city with plenty of hillbillies, but also with more than its share of sophisticates, or cityslickers. This is a Southeastern regional pronunciation and even most of the city's educated and cultured prefer this pronunciation.

EXPESHELLY *adv.* Especially. This is another one of my all time favorite hillbillyisms, which is used way too commonly, even among those who should know better. In October of 1998, I was amazed and amused to actually see this one in print in an Editorial in the Coldwater, Michigan daily newspaper, *The Daily Reporter.* I must confess, however, that they didn't use the "she" part. I firmly believe that it was not a misprint and was actually submitted this way by the columnist and set-up as such by the printer, both of whom, I am convinced, thought this to be the correct spelling, based on the only pronunciation that they had ever encountered.

EXPRESSO *n.* Espresso. Yet another of my personal favorites. I've seen it in print this way in small town convenience stores, where it is whipped up in an automatic whip machine that would make any true Italian connoisseur toss their linguine. At upscale coffeehouses in major cities, where it is prominently and clearly spelled correctly, I have observed a full third of those ordering it, mispronounce it this way. It's just amazing.

EXSCAPE *v.* or *n.* Escape. This is the preferred usage among hillbillies everywhere.

EXSESSABLE *adj.* Accessible. This is not, strictly speaking, a hillbilly only pronunciation, but one that has come into common usage in modern America, due to

45

EXCSCAPE FROM JILE

the penchant for lazy speech on this continent.

EXTRY *adj.* Extra. This pronunciation is becoming less common and was mostly a Northern usage. Many old timers in the Mid-Northern states still will ask for "alittle extry".

EXZASERBATED *v. –past tense.* Exasperated. Those using this one are generally demonstrating their illiteracy or, at the very least, the marginal condition of their literacy. This is most common in the North Central United States and Mid America.

F

FACED *adj.* Fast. Southern, for the most part. This one can be heard every weekend on the television broadcasts of NASCAR races, as in: "Thet ol baw's gottim wun faced rice core."

FAMBLY *n.* Family. This is a hillbilly classic, uttered by hillbillies, wherever they are to be found. The classic line is: "Hiffn she hain't gud enuff fer fambly, she hain't gonna do fer strienjers."

FAR *n* Fire. Mostly a southern pronunciation, even among non-hillbillies, but used elsewhere strictly by hard core hillbillies, as in "wot's yer hurry, whar's the far?"

FAWK *v.* Fuck. This pronunciation is almost always reserved as an expression of disgust or disbelief and is usually said by itself or prefaced only by the word "aw," as in; "aw fawk."

FELLER *n.* A male individual. This one is mostly an oldtimer's expression, used by rural folk far and wide.

FER *adv.* For. This is a very common usage all over as in: "Hiffn ya hain't fer us, yer aggin us."

FERGIT *v.* Forget. To not remember or to neglect. This is a common pronunciation among hillbillies.

FERN *adj.* Foreign. This is a common rural Midwestern and Southern usage, as in: "It ain't a Ford er a Shivvy, but one o M liddel fern jobs."

FERNER *n.* Foreigner. Someone from another country. "They wus tawkin funny, must be sum o M ferners"

FESS UP *phrase.* A request for a confession. A plea to tell the truth about a matter, as in "fess up baw, yew dun stolt thet chicken." Heard far and wide.

FETCH *v.* To go get an item. A very widely used expression, as in: "Baw, go fetch sum faar wood." FETCHT. - *past tense.* "Ah dun fetcht me a handfull o M air goobers."

FEUWD *v.* to feud. Feud. **FEUWDN**. *–intr.* Feuding. A fight between rival families, communities or factions within a community. "Them two famblys is in a feuwd. Y, theys bin a feuwdn fer years." Mostly Southern in origin, but widely used recently and pretty much cliché.

FIGGERIN' *pres.* tense of *v.* Literally translated as figuring, this term denotes any deep thought given to a matter, as in; "Ah bin doin' me sum figgerin'." A very wide usage.

FIGGERT *past tense* of figgerin'. "Y, ta way ah got er figgert, weez gonna kick us sum ayus."

FILL IT *n.* also -*v.* Filet. This is either a strip of meat or fish or the process by which such strip is cut or processed. Paw might advise: "Fill it M air fish." Mostly a Southern and Western pronunciation, but heard spottily elsewhere.

FISTIKATED *adj.* Sophisticated. Meaning wise in the ways of the world or the big city. This is something to not aspire to, as people who have this quality are to be laughed at, looked down upon and pitied. Used very commonly in all regions.

FITHY *adj.* Filthy. Meaning extremely dirty or unwashed. This is mostly Southern and Western, but is used fairly regularly elsewhere, as in: "Thet baw is fithy."

FITTABEETYDE *phrase.* Fit to be tied, meaning very upset. Used

FISTIKATED

widely, as in: "Thet gul was
fittabeetyde."

FITTIN' *pres. tense of v.* To plan.
Planning, Like **FIXIN'**, below,
this denotes a present intention to
do something. This is the
Northern version of this usage, as
in: "Weez a fittin' ta go uptown."

FIXIN' *pres. tense of v.* To plan.
See **FITTIN'**, above. This is the
Southern version of the usage.

FIZU *half a sentence.* If I was [*sic*]
you. . . As in; "Fizu Ahd be puttin
the hurtin' ta thet baw." Now, I
know that the correct way to say
it is; *if I WERE you*, but that
would result in *FIRU*, which,
while every bit as efficient as its
hillbilly cousin, is almost never
uttered by hillbillies, since they

"doan give no damn bout no grammagical rules."

FLAARS *n. –plur.* Flowers. Mostly Southern, but heard among hardcore hillbillies elsewhere. You know the old slogan: "Say it wit flaars."

FLUSTERATED *v.* Frustrated. This usage is heard very widely, but is especially popular in the Midwest and East. This is a personal favorite of the author herein and is highly demonstrative of how those who never read get confused on what the proper spelling is. It seems to be a merging of flustered and frustrated.

FOLLER *v.* Follow. A mostly Southern and Western usage, as in: "Foller me, baws."

FLAARS

FON *adj.* Fine. While originally a strictly Southern usage, this one has found purchase in hillbilly speech in most regions in recent years. A hillbilly man might say: "She shore is wun fon lookin gal."

FONNEL *adj.* Final. Widely used, but almost universally used in the Southeast, even by non-hillbillies, as in: "Ah ainna goin an thet's fonnel."

FONNELLY *adv.* Finally. Used by the same folks that say "fonnel", meaning decisively or at last.

FORBUHFOR *n.* Four wheel drive vehicle or 4X4. This is usually used in reference to a vehicle, but can also be a piece of lumber. This usage is wide and far flung.

FOT *v.* fight. **FOTTIN'** *–intr.* Fighting. Mostly a Southern and

FORBUHFOR

Western usage, but heard elsewhere occasionally. Maw might say: "Yew baws stop thet fottin'."

FOV *n.* Five. The number. This is primarily a Southern pronunciation.

FROD *v.* –*past tense* Fried. Another primarily Southern and Southwestern usage. The classic example is: "frod chicken."

FROTT *n.* Fright. A scare or fear, as in: "Ah had me a terrible frot" or something unsightly, as in: "Ain't yew a frot." Mostly a Southern usage.

FROTTNEN *adj.* Frightening. Indicating a cause of fright. Used by the same crowd as uses Frott, above.

FROTTFULL *adj.* Frightful. Similar usage to the last two entries and used to denote something disgusting or distasteful or to express an extreme. Billy Bob might well exclaim: "Thet there is a frotfull lookin dawg."

FUKKINAY *phrase.* A powerful affirmation. This is used universally by hillbillies and is used either alone or followed by the word rot, meaning right, as in: "Fukkinay rot, Ah dun it."

FURPIECE *contraction* of far and piece, meaning far away. A long journey, as in; "Its a furpiece down thet road ta the big city." This enjoys wide usage, but is most prevalent in the West, South and Midwest.

60

FUSSN *pres tense of v.* To fuss. Fussing. This has a fairly broad meaning in the hillbilly language and not only means fidgeting, but more commonly means creating a scene or acting in a disorderly fashion, similar to **CAREYNON.** This widely used word is very often associated with **FOTTIN,** as in: "M baws was a fussn an a fottin."

FUST *adj.* First. The earliest in time or space or highest in rank or order. This is mostly Southern and Western, but enjoys fairly broad usage. As they say: "Fust thangs fust."

FUTHER *adv.* Farther. To denote a greater literal distance or more distance in space, as in: "its futher then yew mot thank." *-adj.* further for denoting figurative

distance or a greater degree, as
in: "Yew hain't takin this no
futher." Very widely used.

FUTHERMORE *adv.* Furthermore.
Moreover or additionally. Enjoys
the same degree of usage as
FUTHER, above.

FUTWITH *n.* Fort Worth, Texas.
This is the way they pronounce it
there and most places throughout
the Southwest and Mid-South.

G

GAL *n*. Any female, especially a girl friend, as in; "thet's ma gal." A wide usage in all regions, but especially in the South and West.

GAWNA *contraction* of going and to. Cleetus might say, in anger: "Ahma gawna give thet baw a good stompin fer messin round with ma gal." A very common usage, especially in the North and Midwest. See also **GWYNA**, the Southern pronunciation.

GIMME *contraction* of give and me. Give me. Not just heard among hillbillies, but very widely heard indeed.

GIT *v.* Get. Another very common usage everywhere, as in: "ahma gawna git thet baw."

GITGO *v.* or *n.* This is a unique hillbilly usage in all regions which is sumetimes used to describe ambition or a general state of being energetic, as in: "Ma gitgo is paarful this mornin." The more common usage, however, is as a noun to describe a starting point or the beginning, as in: " Thet gal wuz onry rot from the gitgo."

GITCHYA *contraction* of get and you. This is very common among hillbillies everywhere. A prime example is: "Y doancha gitchya sum."

GITTALONG *contraction* of get and along. The ability of one to keep going. If one suffers a leg or back injury, which causes a limp, he is said to have a "hitch in his gittalong." A widely used pronunciation.

GITTUP *n.* An outfit or costume. Another commonly heard hillbilly expression. On a trip to New York City or California, a hillbilly might comment; "Look at the gittup on thet cityslicker."

GIVE *past tense of v.* To give. Gave. While this word is, in fact a proper word in English, it is used by hillbillies to denote the past tense, as well as the present, as in: "Paw give sis a dotted eye fer sassin im."

GOAN *pres. tense* of *v.* to go. Going. Widely used, as in: "Ahma goan uptown."

65

GOOBERS *n.* Peanuts. This is almost exclussively a Southeastern usage, as in; "Pace me M goobers, Paw."

GOODAWL *contraction* of good and old. This is a mostly Southern expression, that is also heard occasionally elsewhere. Jim Bob might say, fondly: "Atnairz a goodawl dawg." This term is also very commonly combined with the word **BAW** to refer to any male over 12 who is considered to be an acceptable individual, as in: "Thet thar Clem, he's a goodawl baw."

GORELICK *n.* Garlic. This primarily Southern pronunciation is also, coincidentally, the actual surname of the Assistant United States Attorney General, under Janet Reno, in the Clinton

Administration. This fact is made more comical by the fact that Mr. Clinton's Vice President was Al Gore, making one wonder, as Ms. Gorelick is a female, if this is how she got the job. In hillbilly speak, however, this word describes the pungent bulbous edible plant.

GORMETTE *n.* Gourmet. This widely used pronunciation is used to describe a connoisseur of fine food or an elegant style of cuisine. In hillbilly parlance, this often means the sort of fare available at a chain buffet restaurant, where "gormette cookin'" is served.

GOSHEATE *v.* Negotiate. This is a hillbilly favorite, which is used far and wide.

GOTDAM *contraction*. Goddamn. This is the preferred hillbilly pronunciation of this particular profanity everywhere.

GOTS *–past tense* and *–past participle* of *v*. to get. Got or have. Its very common to hear hillbillies say that they "gots" something or other.

GOTSTA *contraction* of got and to. Have to or has to. Yes, that's right, a literal translation into English would be "have to" or "has to", but once again, one must bear in mind the hillbilly penchant for abandoning grammar. Children are apt to whine to Maw: "Aw Maw, do we gotsta?"

GRAMMAGICAL *adj*. Grammatical. This wide usage is ironically how redneck types refer to conformity to the rules of grammar. As a rule, though, hillbillies "doan give no damn bout no grammagical rules nohow."

GRANNY *n.* Grandmother. This usage has become cliché, but originated in the Appalachian region of the Southeast, as a classic hillbilly word.

GRANPAPPY *n.* Grandfather. This is a little less cliché than **GRANNY**, but not by much. It's origins are similar as well.

GRAP *v.* Grab. Especially popular usage in the North and Midwest, but heard fairly widely, as in: "Grap me a hanful uv M goobers." **GRAPT**. - *past tense.* Grabbed. As in: "Jew see thet. Y Dixie dun grapt thet gul by the harr O her haid."

GRATCHIATE *n.* Graduate. -*v.* to graduate. Widely used. **GRATCHIATED** - *past tense.* Graduated. Maw an Paw would proudly exclaim: "Y weez so prod O thet baw, He dun gratchiated the eighth grade."

GRIVEY *n.* Gravy. This is primarily a Southern usage. In this word the "i" is pronounced like the word eye. "Grivey" comes in three basic varieties. There's white "milk grivey", often containing ground "poke sawsitch", which is served over "biskits" for breakfast or atop "chicken frod steak" for dinner. There's also "red eye grivey", made from hamhock drippins and served primarily with dinner, which is the hillbilly noon meal and then there's "brown grivey" made with chicken drippins and served over "maisht taiters" for supper, the evening meal.

GRODE *past participle* of Grow. Grown. Used everywhere that hillbillies can be found, as in: "Ah member when he wur jus a liddel feller, but now he's all grode up."

GROM *n.* Grime. Ground in or thickly caked dirt, oil, grease or a combination thereof. This is mostly a Southern pronunciation.

GUBMINT *n.* Government. This is a widely used pronunciation, which is sometimes pronounced **GUMMINT.**

GUL *n.* Girl. Usually denoting a female child and specifically what hillbilly men call their daughters, as opposed to **GAL**, which is

71

usually a "grode woman." Paw might say: "Yew mond yer Paw, gul!"

GWYNA *contraction* of going and to. This is a Deep South usage of **GAWNA**. This probably has its origins in the usage of the African slaves of the old South, which merged into the broader community down through the years. See also **GAWNA**, the Northern equivalent.

H

HAID *n.* Head. Mostly a Southeastern and Mid-South pronunciation. If you anger a hillbilly, they are likely to "thump yer haid."

HAIN'T *contraction* of is not or are not. This pronunciation is most often used when followed by personal pronouns, such as I, they, we, he or she, as in: "Ah hain't gawna take nunna yer shee-ot." See also, **AIN"T**.

HAISH BRONZE *n.* Hash browns. A way of cooking potatoes. This is primarily a Southern pronunciation, which is probably appropriate, since, in my experience, the only place where they know how to cook these properly is in the South. I, personally, call them "hash whites" in the North, since Northerners rarely cook them to the point where they actually turn brown.

HANKERIN' *v.* A desire. This usage is primarily Southern, but is heard fairly often elsewhere. A hillbilly who is hungry might say: "Ah gots me a hankerin' fer sum vittles."

HANNEL *v.* or *n.* Handle. The noun form would be like in a "door hannel", while the verb form might be used as follows: "Ah cain't quite get a hannel on it." This is a widely heard usage.

HANNELLIT *contraction* of handle and it. This is a classic combination, as in: "Jus hannel it." This is heard in most regions, but primarily in the South.

HARR *n.* Hair. Mostly heard in the South and West. When they are referring to the hair on top of ones cranium, hillbillies often will refer to it as: "the harr O the haid."

HARSE *n.* Horse. A large animal often used for pulling objects, such as wagons, buggies or plows and also on which people often ride atop, on a saddle. Mostly a Western pronunciation, but also quite common in the South, with more spotty usage elsewhere.

HAT *v.* –*past tense* of to have. Had. Widely used in all regions. -*adj.* That. This latter usage is almost exclusively a Northern usage, reserved for the beginning of a sentence, as in: "Hat wun'll do."

HATDAWGLEHUNT *contraction* of that dog will hunt. Used as an affirmative response, meaning yes or that something will work. This is a fairly obscure usage, but is heard many places. When expressing that something will suffice, the hard core hillbilly will exclaim; "Hatdawglehunt."

HAWG *n.* Hog or pig. Mostly Southern, but used in an almost cliché manner elsewhere.

HAWG ROTTEN TAITERS *n.* Au gratin potatoes. Another way of cooking "taiters", involving "baikin M" with cheese. Widely used, but fairly obscure.

HAWNTN–*intr. v.* Hunting. This is the Southern version of the word

HAWG

for seeking out prey, from small game, like squirrels and rabbits to larger game, such as deer and "bars". See also **HUNTN**, the Northern usage.

HAYWZ *v.* House. Must be stated in one syllable to work. This is another word heard almost exclusively in the South.

HELT *past tense* of *v.* to hold. *-Past participle*. Held. A common pronunciation in all regions. An example is: "Theyz helt ta a higher stannert."

HEYUEEL *contraction* of the hell you will. This is another widely used expression, which must be said with great defiance in response to any threat.

HIFFN *conj.* If. Used to introduce a subjective, negative conditional,

78

indirect question or exclamatory clause. Also meaning on condition that or to express surprise or anger. -*n*. A possibility, condition or stipulation. This is the preferred pronunciation in the North, especially when used at the beginning of a sentence. See also **IFFN**.

HITCH IN YER (IZ, ER) GITTALONG *Expression*. Rodeo contestants often suffer from this condition, according to TV commentators of that sport. After a fall from a bull or bucking bronco, the commentator will exclaim: "Well, thet awlbawz gots im a hitch in iz gittalong." See also **GITTALONG.**

HITCHT *n*. to wed. Hitched. To get married at a ceremony. This enjoys very wide usage, as in:

79

"they dun gots hitch." See also
MARJ.

HOEDOWN *n*. A really big party.
Usually indicating a party
involving a country band, Bar B
Que and "lottsa" beer. Mostly
used in the South and West, but
heard elsewhere, just with less
frequency.

HOLLER *n*. A mountain valley, as
in: "We live jus up the holler."
This particular usage is
indigenous almost exclusively to
the mountains of Appalacia in the
Southeast. -*v*. to yell. This usage
is much less regional and is heard
far and wide, as in: "Hiffn ya
need anythang, jus give a holler."
HOLLERT *v*. –*past tense* Yelled.

HOLT *v*. To hold. Used widely, this
word can be heard in a "marj"

ceremony, when the preacher says the bit about "to have and to holt, til death do yew port."

HOOEEE *exclamation.* An expression of joy. This is mostly a Southern and Western expression, which must be "hollert" with great enthusiasm.

HOOPLAW *n.* a fuss or a ruckus. When there is some sort of general pandemonium going on, a hillbilly would say: "Whats all the hooplaw bout?"

HOOTNANNY *n.* A major celebration, usually one even larger than the average "hoedown" and usually involves live music. This is another primarily Southern usage, indicating a community wide party, such as a barn dance or community picnic.

HOWDY *interj.* Hello. This is the standard hillbilly greeting, throughout the known hillbilly world and while it probably originated in the traditional hillbilly regions of the South, it has become cliché everywhere, as in "Howdy, Strinejer. Have yersef a sitdown. Tike yer shoes off. Yawl come baick now, hear?"

HOYPOLLOY *n.* Superior acting persons of wealth and high social standing, who look down on hillbillies. See also **HOYTITOYTI**. See also **HYFALUTTIN'**, which is the attitude of the "Hoypolloy".

HOYTITOYTI *adj.* Meaning an attitude indicating superiority, as in: "Well, doan she thank she's jus all hoytitoyti." This describes the attitude displayed by the

HOYPOLLO. Also *n*. Referring to a person or group who displays an attitude of superiority, as in: "Theyz among the hoytitoyti." This is primarily Southern, but is heard elsewhere occasionally.

HUN *n*. Short for honey, as in darling, as a term of endearment. This is widely used by hillbilly women and most especially by waitresses in truck stops and rural diners. The classic example is when a waitress, named Flo or Pearl, says; "Wot kin ah git ya, hun?" This originated in the South, but thanks to television, has spread like wildfire throughout North America and has become cliché.

HUNNERT *n*. Hundred. This is another word that displays the hillbilly penchant for converting

83

the letter D into a T sound. This is a very widely used pronunciation.

HUNTN *–intr. v.* Hunting. This is the way it is pronounced throughout the Northern reaches of the hillbilly world. See also **HAWNTN**, the Southern usage.

HUNTNDAWG *contraction* of hunting and dog. This can either be a direct reference to a canine that is trained and suitable for use in hunting birds and animals, or can be used to proclaim some item to be fit generally for some purpose. As an example of the latter usage, when declaring an item suitable for some task, Clem might well state: "Atnairza huntndawg," meaning that it will work. This is fairly common, but generally only among hard core

rural hillbillies. See also
HATDAWGLEHUNT.

HURT *past tense* of *v.* to hear.
Heard. Another widely used
pronunciation of T in place of D,
as in the common affirmation:
"Ah hurt thet", Meaning that one
is in agrement.

HYFALUTTIN' *adj.* This is similar
to HOYTITOYTI, but is less
regional and conveys more an
attitude or general air about a
person who considers themself to
be socially or financially
superior.

I

IDBE *contraction* of it would be. This widely heard standard is the ultimate in passive voice, don't you think?

IDEAL *n.* Idea. The product of the hillbilly mind or the formation of a thought, which itself, is a major effort for hillbillies. Billy Joe Jim Bob is likely to say: "Ah gots me an ideal."

IFFN *adj.* If. This is the preferred usage of the word if in the South or when used mid-sentence in other regions, as in: "Yew kin do it iffn ya wanna." See also **HIFFN**.

IKE *v.* Ache. To suffer or be in pain. **IKEN, IKT** *–intr.* This is primarily heard in the South, as in "Ah gots an iken in ma heart." *-n.* A dull steady pain. Combined with the hillbilly word for head, you get "haidike".

INNERST *n.* or *v.* Interest. A cause of curiosity or wonderment or a right or claim to something. Also a payment or charge. **INNERSTIN** *–tr. v.* to cause curiosity or interest in, as in: "Thet shore is innerstin."

INNIT *contraction* of is it not, as in: "Thet's one helluva core, innit?" This form of the usage has its roots in Great Britain, where it is actually more prevalent, but it is also heard in many parts of North American, especially in the East and South. *-contraction* of in and it. This is a very common usage everywhere.

IM *pron.* Him. This is another example of economy of language, as practiced by hillbillies far and wide.

IMSELF *pron.* Himself. Widely used, as in: "Baw gots imself innit deep."

IRREGARDLESS *adj.* Regardless. For some unfathomable reason, there is an increasing trend, even among non-hillbillies, who should definitely know better, to want to ad an "ir" at the beginning of a perfectly good word. This is a shockingly common phenomenon, which I find quite surprising, as it is less economical that the correct usage.

ITE *n.* Eight. The number eight, as pronounced primarily in the South.

IZ *poss.* form of *pron.* he. His. This particular usage is limited to certain instances where it is to be used in mid-sentence, like in: "Ahmoan kick iz ayuss." This is also the standard pronunciation of the word "is", not only by hillbillies, but by most English speaking people.

J

JAWJAH *n*. Georgia, the Southern U S State.

JES *Adv*. Just. Meaning precisely, as in: "Thet's jes the way it is", or barely, as in: "Yew jes missed it", or at the exact moment, as in: "It's jes noon." Widely used.

JEWEET? *contraction* of did you eat? This is common, even among non-hillbillies as a lazy way of uttering this query in the interest of verbal economy.

JEWNO *contraction* of did you know. A lazy pronunciation developed through years of slothfulness and used so widely that it can be heard among those who certainly know better. "Jewno what I done hurt bout M folks?"

JILE *n.* Jail. This is primarily a Southern pronunciation and is a place that most hillbillies spend at least some time and many spend most of their lives there. This is not, strictly speaking, limited to County Jail, but hillbillies usually refer to prisons as "jile."

JITTERY *adj.* Nervous or unsettled. This one is fairly commonly heard throughout all regions among the less eloquent sector. Upon noticing a friend fidgeting, one might say: "Wot R yew all jittery bout."

JWANNA *contraction* of do you want to. Another of the slothful, verbally economical utterances that are heard, not just among

hillbillies, but far and wide, as
in: "Jwanna go grap a beer after
work?"

K

K *n.* O.K. or okay. Meaning satisfactory. An approval, endorsement or affirmation. Very widely esed as in "K, Ah'll dew it."

KACKELATE *v.* To calculate and in Hillbilly parlance, to think about or figure something.
KACKELATEN, KACKELATIT – *intr.* A hillbilly may state: "Y, ta way Ah gots er kackelatit, weez a gawna be gittin outta here soon."

KATTYWOMPUS *adj.* Out of kilter. This is the most common pronunciation of this widely used hillbillyism, however, Some Southerners prefer **KITTYWAUMPUS**. This condition often results in a "hitch in yer

93

gittalong." This is a common usage among the rodeo set. See also **KITTYWAUMPUS**.

KICKAYUS *adj.* Kick ass Awesome or extremely impressive. A widely used expression, as in: "Thet core's got a kickayus motor innit?" Also *v.* This expression can also refer to beating up, as in "ahma gawna kickayus."

KILT *past tense* of *v.* to kill. Killed. This is a very widely used pronunciation, especially in the South, as in: "Thet po baw gots imsef kilt." This is another classic example of the hillbilly penchant for replacing "ed" at the end of a word with a "t" sound.

KIN *n.* Family. This is mostly a Southern usage, but is heard among hard core hillbillies elsewhere as well. Rednecks often refer to any member of their family tree, within 4 to 6 degrees as their "kin". See also **FAMBLY.**

KINNYGARDEN *n.* Kindergarten. The first year of school for children, attended for the School year prior to the first grade.

KITS *n. –plur.* Kids. Paw might say to Maw: "Tell M kits ta shut up er Ah'll bitch slayup M." Mostly Southern, but used fairly commonly in the North and Midwest as well. See also **YUNGUNZ**.

KITTYWAUMPUS *adj.* This is a far more obscure Southern pronunciation of "kattywompus." See also **KATTYWOMPUS**, above.

KRAFT *n*. Carrafe. This is an alternate spelling of **CRAFT**. It means a container for wine. See also **CRAFT**, above.

KRINE *–intr. v.* Crying. A mostly Southern, but fairly common usage generally, as in: "Aw stop thet krine."

<u>L</u>

LAIST *adj.* or *–intr. v.* Last. The final one in a series, as in: "Thet's the laist wun." Also a reference to endurance, as in: "Ah shore hope this fun laists fer a spell." This is primarily, but not exclusively, a Southern pronunciation.

LEMME *contraction* of let and me. Let me. This is so widely used that it can not be said to be limited to hillbillies, as in: "Lemme see."

LENTH *n.* Length. A measure of distance or degree. This is heard almost universally in the Southeast and spottily elsewhere. Nascar announcers speak of "corelenths" when describing how much of a lead a racer has. In the hardware store, Jeb would ask for a "lenth O rope."

LERNIN' *pres tense* of *n.* to learn. Learing. The acquisition of knowledge or skills. An education. "Thet bawz got im sum lernin'." Originated and most prevalent in the South, but widely used elsewhere as cliché.

LERNT *v.* –*past tense* of to learn. Usage is the same as **LERNIN**, above, but less cliché. Paw would say: "Ah dun lernt thet gul ta lie ta me by givin her a good whuppin'."

LICKER *n.* Liquor. To be totally fair, this is the way most North Americans pronounce this, but it just looks so hokey spelled this way, it had to be included.

LICKERT *adj.* Drunk. Meaning intoxicated by alcoholic beverages, or liquor. This is a common way to refer to the state of intoxication by alcohol, as in: "Thet sumbitch iz lickert aggin."

LIDDEL *adj.* Little. Meaning small in size or in quantity or degree. Widely used, as in: "Gimme a liddel O thet stuff."

LIONIZED *adj.* Lyonnaise. Meaning cooked with onions. Hillbillies refer to potatoes cooked with onions, and usually with cheese, in this manner, as "lionized potatoes." I have actually seen this in print on menus more than once.

LOLLYGAGGIN' *v.* Lounging or procrastinating. This usage, which is widely heard, usually indicates a sort of standing about, wasting time, as opposed to "settin' 'round." Maw might yell: "Yew yungunz hurry up an git rhettago an stop thet lollygaggin', yawl hear?"

LON *n.* Line. This is almost exclusively a Southern pronunciation.

LON DANSIN' *v.* Line dancing. This is a favorite pastime of hillbillies far and wide, which involves a group of rednecks, men dressed in blue jeans, cowboy boots and cowboy hats, women dressed in frilly skirts, doing synchronized dances to the most God-awful noise you've ever

LOLLYGAGGIN

heard, which they refer to as "country music."

LONDRY *v.* or *n.* Laundry. This is mostly a Northern and Western pronunciation, while Southerners tend more towards **LAWNDREY**.

LOOKEELOU *n.* This specifically means one who stares rudely at some thing or event. Most often these are seen slowing their vehicles to a crawl when passing an automobile accident.

LOOKIE *v.* Look. This is not only used by hillbillies, but also by those annoying people that use cutsie talk, as in: "Lookie here."

LOOZYANNA *n.* Louisiana. A Southern state along the North shore of the Gulf of Mexico and home to a wide variety of rednecks and hillbillies, as well

102

as some surprisingly sophisticated
people. This is also the only state
in the US that observes French
Common Law, as opposed to
English Common Law, which is
observed in the other 49 states.

LOT *n.* or *v.* Light. Mostly a
Southern pronunciation, the verb
is used as in: "Ah'll lot the way."
The noun is used to refer to a
point of light or a lighting
fixture.

LOVERLY *adj.* Lovely. Something
attractive or pleasant to behold. A
widely used word, as in: "Hain't
she jes a loverly liddel thang."

LYBARRY *n.* Library. This
mispronunciation is another one
of those that is heard appallingly
often, even among those who
clearly should know better, as in:

"Ah dun seen it at the lybarry."
This is not a place frequented by
the trailer park set, however.

LYTER *comparitive* of *adj*. Late.
Mostly Southern, but fairly
widely heard elsewhere, as in:
"See yawl lyter."

LYER *n*. Lawyer. This is the
Southern pronunciation of the
other word for attorney and is, to
the best of my knowledge purely
coincidental, as in "Ah hired me a
lyer ta git me a deevorse." Don't
even bitch to me if this offends
you, since I am, myself, a lawyer.

M

M *pron.* Them or *plur.* of *adj.* that; those. The latter usage is by far the most common hillbilly usage, as they never use the word THOSE, choosing instead to use this shortened form of the word THEM. "M dawgs is maikin an awful fuss."

M R *contraction* of them are. I know it should be *those are*, but remember, these are hillbillies we're talking about here. This is widely used and often seen in the famous little word gag containing the exchange: "M R ducks. M R not. R 2. L I B, M R ducks."

M AIR *contraction* of them there. Once again, I know it should be

105

those there, but again I wish to point out, this is hillbilly grammar, not the kings English. Jethro might exclaim: "Y lookie M air."

MA *poss.* form of *Pron.* I. My This is predominately a Southern pronunciation, but is used elsewhere occasionally. See also **MAW** for the Western pronunciation. Also *pron.* Mother. This usage is mostly Northern, while southerners prefer **MAW**.

MAISH *v.* Mash. This predominately Southern usage can have the traditional meaning or can mean to push down or press, as in a key or button. "Jus maish rot daywn on it." **MAISHT** *–past tense.* Mashed.

MAISHT TAITERS *n.* Mashed potatoes. A way of preparing potatoes by pulverizing them with milk and butter, as in: "Weez havin frod chicken with maisht taiters n grivey fer supper."

MAITERS *n. plural* Tomatoes. This is a fairly widely used pronunciation, but is most prevalent in the South. "Pace me M maiters."

MARJ *n.* Marriage. The state of being husband and wite or of being married. Also the ceremony of marriage. See also **HITCHT**.

MAW *poss.* form of *pron.* I. My (Western). This usage is fairly obscure and heard primarily among the mountain folk of the Western US Rockies. See also **MA**. -*n.* Mother. This is primarily

MARJ OR HITCHT

Southern, at least in its origins, but has become pretty cliché.

MAYWTH *n*. Mouth. This is another Southern word that must be said in one syllable. Piss off a hillbilly and they'll say: "Ahma gawna smaish yer maywth."

MEMBER *v*. Remember. This is mostly a Northern and Mid-Western usage, which represents another economy of verbage, as in: "Ah cain't rotly member thet."

MESS *n*. A large quantity or amount. This widely used word can function to describe a whole range of items, people or things that have great quantity. When the word "whole" precedes this one, it describes a truly huge quantity. Some common examples are: "A mess O taiters": or "A whole mess O kits."

MISSOURAH *n.* The state of Missouri. Also known as the "Show Me State," whatever the hell that means. I do know, however, that in the state of Missouri, it is firmly believed that; "nothin' beats a goodal Missourah mule." There are, by the way, a "whole mess O hillbillies" in that particular state. There are lots of trailer parks there too.

MON *Poss. pron.* Mine. Southern in origin, but widespread now, this is the preferred hillbilly pronunciation, as in: " Git yer fithy hands offn thet, it's mon."

MOND *n.* Mind. The noun form, as in the terrible thing to waste, is a lesser usage among hillbillies. *-v.* This is the more common usage, meaning to obey, as in: "Yew yungunz mond yer maw." Also meaning to Pay attention to, as in: "Mond yew doan git all Kattywompus n gitchya a hitch in yer gittalong."

MOT *adj.* Might, usually meaning mighty or expressing an extreme. This Southern pronunciation is often combined with the hillbilly word, **PARFULL**, to indicate a strong feeling or desire, as in: "Ah gots me a mot parfull hankerin' fer sum viddels."

MUNTS *n.* Months. The 12 major divissions of a year on a calender. Widely used as in: "Ah ain't seen im fer munts."

N

N M *contraction* And them. This is a very common usage in all regions, as in: "Ahma goan ta the store with Maw N M." This word, in print, should not be confused with the postal code for New Mexico.

NAIRY *adj.* None at all. The usage of this word is similar to the words BARELY and HARDLY, except that this word indicates not just a few, but none. This is largely a Southern and Mid-States usage, as in: "We went fishin', but dihunt catch nairy a wun."

NARLINS *n.* New Orleans. A city in Louisianna. A very popular place among folks from all walks

112

of life. Home of the Blues, Cajun
Cooking and endless decadence
and crime.

NAWTH *n.* North. This is a strictly
Southern Pronunciation, which is
carried further with the usage
NAWTHUN, meaning Northern.
See also **NORT** and **NORDERN**,
for the northern pronunciation.

NAYZCORE *n.* NASCAR. National
Association for Stock Car Auto
Racing. An automobile racing
organization that puts on racing
events throughout the United
States. These events are
collectively witnessed first hand
by millions of hillbillies and are
watched on television by tens, if
not hundreds of millions. These
events are run in serial fashion
with each series having a major
tobacco company or brewery

sponsoring the series, consisting
of individual races sponsored by
other companies, usually in the
tobacco, beer, fast food or auto
parts and services business. The
most popular of these series are
the Winston Cup series, followed
by the Busch series. In each
series the same 45 to 50 drivers
compete against each other in one
of two US manufacturers' product,
Ford or GM (GM is broken down
into Chevrolet, Pontiac and
Oldsmobile, but these cars are
really all the same) that are
driven around an oval for 200 to
500 miles, while banging into
each other. These events are a
central theme in hillbilly life and
most hillbillies have passionate
feelings about the drivers that go
up against one another week after
week. "Nayzcore" is the Deep

South, Mid-South and Southeastern pronunciation, while among most Northern, Mid-Western and Western hillbillies it is simply pronounced NAZCAR.

NEEVER *adj.* also –*pron.* *-adv.* or *-conj.* Neither. Not one or the other. Usually used in adjective or pronoun form, as in: "Neever wun suits me." Most commonly used by hillbillies, however as the Adverb "not", as a double negative, as in: "ah dihunt neever dew it." This usage is widespread.

NEWFANGLED *adj.* Modern. This is a largely cliché word with roots in the Appalachian region which usually indicates some newly developed, complicated contraption, as in "Ah cain't figger out how ta use M air newfangled computers."

NOCKED UP *adj.* Pregnant. This is the most common way to refer to someone becoming pregnant. It is also quite often used to define the state of being pregnant, but the latter use is most common when it is being expressed in a derogatory fashion. While Paw would normally express that "at gul dun got hersef nocked up," it would only be with disgust that he would say: "She's nocked up." If not disgusted, he would more likely say: "She's pregnut" See also PREGNUT.

NODE *past tense* of *v.* to know. Knew. This is a hard core hillbilly usage, as in: "Ah node it, I just dun node it."

NOHOW *contraction* of what should be no and way or any and way, but gets translated into trailer park talk as no and how. This is a classic hillbilly expression, which is usually said in all regions as part of a double negative, as in: "It doan make no diffurnz nohow."

NON *n.* Nine. Originally a strictly Southern pronunciation, this one is heard fairly often in other regions as well.

NORT *n.* North. This is the far Northern pronunciation, which is expanded into **NORDERN**, meaning Northern. See also **NAWTH** and **NAWTHUN** for the Southern pronunciation.

NORT KACKLACKEY *n.* North Carolina. This is a US state along the Atlantic Coast. This is a regional pronunciation, which is generally only heard in the

Carolinas. See also **SOU'**
KACKLACKEY

NOSS *adj.* Nice. An almost
exclusively Southern
pronunciation meaning pleasant.

NOSSLY *adv.* Nicely. Also
primarily a Southern
pronunciation meaning done in a
satisfactory manner. Maw might
say: "Thet baw dun rot nossly fer
iseff."

NUHUH *adv.* or –*adj.* No. This is
used by hillbillies as a negative
response to an inquiry. This far
flung usage must be said in two
quick syllables with the second
beginning with a guttural sound.
This is usually a stand alone
word.

NUN *n.* None. Indicating zero or lack of quantity. Wide usage. See also **Nairy**.

NUNNA *contraction* of none and of, as in: "It hain't nunna yer damn bidness." This is common in all regions.

NUNDER *contraction* of in and under. This is a usage peculiar to the Mid-West and North. It is particularly common in the Southern Great Lakes and Ohio Valley. When moving the house trailer to a new location, Cleetus would say: "Jes slide M wheels nunder thar n we'll be a movin' this thang."

NUTHER *n.* Neither. Another wide usage everywhere, as in: "Tain't nuther wun er the other."

O

OFFN *contraction* of off and of or off and from. An example of this multi-regional usage would be: "Git thissear thang offn me."

OL'BAW *contraction* of old and boy. This is largely Southern in origin, but has crept into usage elsewhere and has even become quasi-cliché. "Thet Billy Bob cracks me up. Thet ol'baw shore do know how ta tell a joke." Often this is preceded by the word "good". See also **GOODAWLBAW**.

ONRY *adj.* Ornery. While the true definition, in English, is mean spirited or to have a mean disposition, in hillbilly parlance

120

it is more indicative of being feisty or rowdy. This is often meant as a quasi-complimentary term, as in: "Weeunz is onry."

OSS *n.* Ice. Frozen water. This is largely Southern, but is heard occasionally elsewhere.

OVERHAWLS *n.* Overalls. This is a piece of apparel worn by rural hillbillies and farmers. There are basically two major varieties; blue denim or tan. These two varieties are often identified with reference to the major manufacturers of each variety; the former are "Levi's overhawls," while the latter are "Carhardt overhawls."

OVERTA *contraction* of over and to. This is an extremely common usage, especially in the North, which can mean literally what it says, as in: "Ahma goan overta Maw's" or can indicate a location, as in: "Ah left ma core overta Maw's." The latter usage replaces the word "at" in many situations.

OWN *prep.* On. Indicating position or placement atop or in contact with. This is pretty much strictly Southern, as in: "Git own wit it."

OWNY *adj.* Only. Alone or one of a kind. A lone item. See also **OWNYUS**, below for the expession denoting extreme loneness.

OWNYUS *expression.* The only one. This is a hard core Southern and Appalachian usage, which indicates a total lack of any thing or item of like kind anywhere and takes the word **OWNY** to the furthest degree. This expresses an absolute lack of duplication. Old Jeb might say: "Thet thar gal wuz ta ownyus wun wot ever dun made me feel thetaway." See also **OWNY**, above.

PILLER

P

PACE *v*. Pass. This is primarily a Southern pronunciation, which is regularly uttered by TV commentators of NASCAR races. Ned Jarret will say: "Dayal better look out, cause Jeff Gordon's Fixin ta pace him on the outsod."

PAH *n*. Pie. This is not only a widely used pronunciation, which grew out of the South into very broad usage, but is also an absolute favorite food of hillbillies and North Americans in general.

PAPPY *n*. Father or Dad. This word usage originated in the South and West, but is heard elsewhere. This usage has become fairly rare and obscure in recent years.

124

PATICALUR *adj.* Particular. Belonging to a specific thing, person or group. Separate and distinct. Exceptional or noteworthy, as in: Ah'll tike thet paticalur wun." Also *n.* Indicating a specific thing, person or group, as in: "Wot er yer paticalurs." The fromer use is by far more common among hillbillies than the latter and is heard in all regions.

PARFULL *adj.* Powerful. In actual hillbilly usage this is more likely used in place of strong. Mostly a Southern pronunciation, it is often preceded by the hillbilly word MOT, as in a "mot parfull hankerin'."

PAW *n. informal* Father. This almost cliché hillbillyism has its roots in the traditional hillbilly country of the Appalachians and

Ozarks, but has spread like wildfire elsewhere, as in: "Thet's ma Paw." One of my favorite cliché uses is contained in an old song by Arthur Godfrey, which cun still be found in flea markets and antique shops, titled: "Slap her down aggin, Paw." The author actually has a copy of this gem, which he cherishes.

PAYST *past tense v.* to pass. Passed. This is the traditional Nascar or highway driving usage. Also *-adj.* Past. Mostly Southern, but heard quite often elsewhere, as in: "Thet's all in the payst."

PENCIL PUSHER *n.* Any office worker. This means "wunna M gotdam college boys upta the office." Widely used among laborers, especially in large, unionized, industrial companies.

126

PIE-ANNA *n.* Piano. This hard core hillbilly usage is used fairly widely, as in: "Thet awlbaw shore kin play thet pie-anna."

PILLER *n.* Pillow. A soft stuffed textile bag for laying ones head upon while sleeping or resting.

PINE *n.* Pain. A primarily Southern pronunciation. Also *v.* to pine or long for. **PINEN** *–intr.* A longing, as in: "Ah gots a pinen fer ya dorlin."

PITCHER *n.* Picture. This is another favorite usage of the wrong word being used to define an item. This misusage is heard regularly among hillbillies and others in the less educated elements of society. Look at a hillbilly and he's liable to say: "Wot yew stairin et baw? Y doncha tike a pitcher? It'll laist longer."

POELEASE *n.* Police. **POELEASES** *–plur.* This pronunciation has Southern roots in the merging of slang among the races, but in modern times it is common among all sorts of demographics, as in: "Wawtch out fer the poelease" or "The Poeleases are a comin'."

POKE *n.* Pork. This is the Southern pronunciation for pork, but is also a multi-regional, more obscure term for a sack, usually a gunny sack, as in "A pig in a poke." I suppose that if you butchered that pig and put him back in the sack and were in the South, you would have "Poke in a poke."

PORK *v.* to park. Park **PORKT** – *past tense.* Parked. **PORKIN** –

POELEASE

pres. tense. Parking. *-n.* Park. The verb usage means to leave an automobile in a spot. This is a strictly Southern pronunciation, as in: "Ah porkt the core overta the pork " The noun is used to describe an open outdoor space or place of public recreation, as in: "Ahma goan ta the pork with Maw N M."

PORT *n.* Part. This pronunciation is heard in the South, especially the Southwest. In Texas, for example, they refer to car parts as "core ports."

POSTA *contraction* of supposed and to. Supposed to. This is a multi-regional usage, as in: "Paw sayd yer posta git wood."

PREESHYATE *v.* Appreciate. Usually in hillbilly speech this is an expression of gratitude, as in: "Ah shore do preshyate it," but can also mean to go up in value or to express admiration. Widely used.

PREGNUT *adj.* Pregnant. This is the result of getting "nocked up." See also **NOCKED UP**

PRIVY *n.* Outhouse. These are outdoor facilities for relieving oneself of bodily waste and are becoming more rare, but still are in everyday use among the poorest of rural hillbillies, who aren't wealth enough to buy a trailer with indoor plumbing. These structures are free-standing shanties, usually about 4 feet by 6 feet in footprint with a back sloping roof, placed over a pit for collecting the waste and usually having a two hole bench. This

131

PRIVY

variety is called a "two-holer", in which the second whole is not so much for sharing the experience, as for when the weather turns cold, at which time a crumpled up piece of paper can be ignited and dropped down the adjacent hole to warm the seat.

PROD *adj.* Proud. Originating in the South, this pronunciation is also heard quite frequently elsewhere, as in "Maw and Paw shore R prod O M yungunz."

PROLLY *adv.* Probably. This is another foreshortened form of the correct word that is heard commonly in trailer parks among hillbillies everywhere.

PROLLUM *n.* Problem. Heard widely throughout North America, as in: "Wots yer prollum, baw."

PROM *adj.* Prime. Meaning of the first quality or foremost, as in: "M's some prom viddels." -*v.* To prepare or make ready. This is a less common hillbilly usage but might be heard in certain contexts, such as: "Prom the pump, soze the wawter'll cum a runnin'." Almost exclusively a Southern pronunciation.

PROPER *adv.* Properly. While it is true that the word "proper" is indeed a proper adjective in the English language, hillbillies use it in the adverb form, which properly should be "properly." It is also used as an adverb to denote sufficiency, as in: "Paw dun whupt thet baw proper." This usage is multi-regional.

PURFUR *v.* Prefer. This is an example of the hillbilly

134

preference for re-organizing words. This is another widely heard pronunciation.

PURTEE *adj.* Pretty. Another example of word re-organization, this one is also heard in all localities where hillbillies are found, as in: "She shore is a purty liddel thang."

PURTNEER *adv.* Almost. This usage is mostly Northern, Midwestern and Western, but is also heard elsewhere occasionally. The origins of this word come from the settlers who moved west to stake their claims merging the expression "pretty near" to denote proximity to a destination, as in: "It's purtneer tom ta go uptaywn with Maw N M." It has since been expanded to denote nearness in

time, as well as space. As in:
"Weez purtneer thar."

Q

QUADDER *n.* Quarter. This is widely heard in rural areas, usually in reference to the monitary denomination, as in: "Wot ta hell, it owny costs ya a Quadder." Sometimes this is further shortenned into simple a **QUAD**.

R

R *poss.* form of *pron.* We. Our. Also
–*pres, tense* of *v.* to be. Are.
While the latter usage is actually
the pronunciation used by nearly
all English speaking people, it is
worthy of note here, by way of
pointing out its verbal economy
for written uses like: "M R" or
"we R." This economical usage
has now been made famous by
"Toys R Us," which further makes
use of a backwards "R," just to
further confuse hillbillies and in
order to make the upcoming
generation even more illiterate
than the last, if that is possible.
The former usage is quite common
among Americans generally, not
just hillbillies, as only the most

proper, literate Americans
actually annunciate the "ou"
sound anymore.

RAHFFIL *n.* Rifle. A firearm with a
long barrel with spiral grooves
inside and a stock to be placed
against the shoulder, which shoots
a projectile from a cartridge
propelled by gunpowder. Used by
hillbillies for **HUNTN**.

RASSLIN' *–pres. tense* of *v.* to
wrestle. Wrestling. This is a
hillbilly classic, which in its less
common usage, denotes a sport
that is engaged in among student
athletes, however, its more
common usage, among trailer park
types, indicates a professional
sport, which is a favorite among
hillbillies, along with NASCAR
racing and rodeo. The
professional sport of "rasslin'"

RASSLIN'

involves very large men acting out fights in a ring, while wearing ridiculous and gaudy outfits, which is clearly phony and acted out to anybody except most hillbillies, who truly believe that it is genuine and athletic. While it is true that some athletic ability is necessary to partake in this activity and indeed those partaking can not avoid the occasional injury, professional wrestling is actually more ballet dancing than actual fighting.

REEYABS *n. plural* Ribs. This word must be pronounced all in one syllable. This denotes not so much a part of vertebrate mammal anatomy as it does a food. In the Southeast this indicates Pork ribs, while in Texas and the West it indicates Beef ribs. In all regions the ribs, of any variety, must be prepared over an open flame and slathered with Bar-B-Que sauce, which is a conglomeration of tomato sauce, vinegar, molasses and spices. This word must be crammed into a single syllable for the proper affect. This is the standard pronunciation across the entire South.

REGLUR *adj.* Regular. Normal, average, commonplace or mundane. Also means steady or a constant. This is heard in all hillbilly regions.

RETARD *v.* Retired. This is a Southern usage, meaning that one has ceased their working career. Many hillbillies spend most of their lives in this condition.

RETCHT *past tense* of *v.* to reach. Reached. Another classic example of the hillbilly penchant for replacing the "ed" sound at the end of a word with a "t" sound. This one is heard far and wide, as in: "Ah retcht rot out an grapt thet sumbitch by the haar O the haid."

RHETTAGO *contraction* of ready to go. This is primarily a Northern and Midwestern usage, but is heard spottily elsewhere. This is a Northern hillbilly classic.

RICIN' *–pres. tense* of *v.* to race. Racing. This is pretty much exclusively a Southern usage, which in nearly every instance can mean only one thing: automobile racing and furthermore, almost always means

the hillbilly favorite:
"NAYZCORE Ricin'."

ROM *n.* or *v.* Rhyme or to rhyme. A phonetic similarity in pentameter, as in some forms of poetry. Of course most hillbillies believe that poetry must rhyme. If you read them some T.S. Elliot, they'll likely say: "Who ta hell yew foolin? Thet ain't no poetry. Hell it doan even rom."

ROONT *–past tense* of *v.* to ruin. Ruined. Here again we have the "t" sound replacing "ed" at the end of a word, which is in wide usage among hillbillies everywhere.

ROT *adj.* *–v. archaic* Right. This is the pronunciation for all forms of the word right, including the adjective and verb forms, but in hillbilly speech it is very common to hear the archaic form, as in: "He dun rot nossly." Southern in origin, but heard elsewhere from time to time.

ROTCHAIR *contraction* of right and there. This is a widely used pronunciation among hillbillies, which is used even more widely in the South, even among educated folk. A Southerner will tell you to "Pork it rotchair."

ROTCHEER *contraction* of right and here. This is another Southern usage like the immediately preceding entry, above, as in: Ah wuz rotchair, but now Ahma rotcheer.".

ROTLY *adv.* Rightly. In hillbilly parlance this usually means to be within ones rights or properly

belonging to, as in: "Thet thar gal
is rotly mine."

<u>S</u>

SAAR *adj.* Sour. This pronunciation originated in the South and is used extensively among all people there, but is also used quite commonly among hillbillies elsewhere.

SAAR MAISH *n.* Sour mash whiskey. This is the liquor of choice, especially among Southeastern hillbillies. There are commercially available varieties, but the true Southern redneck either makes his own or gets it from some neighbor or kin who makes it with their own still. The homemade variety is also called "moonshine" or "corn licker."

SAMMICH *n.* Sandwich. This widely used word is also

sometimes pronounced
"sambitch." Maw will send the
"yungunz off ta school wit a ham
sammich."

SAN BERDOO *n.* San Bernardino,
California. There are, of course
many places, which have their
own hillbilly pronunciations, but
hillbillies are not extremely
common in Southern California,
so it is worthy of note to point
out this particular hillbilly
enclave in that region and its
pronunciation among its residents
and those who frequent it.
Appropriately, many of the trailer
park in Southern California are in
and around the San Berdoo area.

SANGIN' *pres. tense* of *v.* to sing.
Singing. Another outgrowth of the
South, this one is also heard quite
commonly elsewhere these days.

SASS TAWK *v.* To talk to one in a disrespectful or insubordinate manner. This usually indicates a child talking back to a parent, teacher or other adult in a position of authority, but can be anybody speaking to one in a superior or authoritarian capacity in a disrespectful way. When the "yungunz argy" with Paw he hollers: "Doanchew yunguns give me no sass tawk er Ah'll give yew a whuppin'." This usage is heard in all hillbilly regions.

SATISTICK *n.* Statistic. **SATISTIX** *–plural* This is a common hillbilly pronunciation everywhere.

SAWSITCH *n.* Sausage. Primarily a Southern pronunciation, this one is also heard quite frequently elsewhere. The most common use for this item is "sawsitch grivey,"

which is served for breakfast with
biscuits.

SAWTURD *v.* Sautéed. A way of
cooking quickly in an open pan in
very hot oil. This is a common
hillbilly usage, which is said with
the emphasis on the first syllable.

SAYD *past tense* of *v.* to say. Said.
Originating in the South, this
pronunciation is now heard very
widely among hillbillies, as in:
"Yew hurt wot Ah sayd."

SEED *past tense* of *v.* to see. Saw.
This is the hard core hillbilly
version of the more popular
SEEN. See below.

SEEN *past tense* of *v.* to see. Saw.
Of course in proper English this
is also a word, but in the correct
usage it is the past participle,
while among the trailer park set it
150

is misused as the regular past tense, as in "Ah dun seen it."

SENSUOUS *contraction* of since you was. As in the classic line: "Sensuous up, wanna grap me a beer." Of course to be grammatically correct, it should be since you *were* or *are* up, but remember, hillbillies "doan give no shee-ot 'bout no grammagical rules."

SET *v.* Sit. A common usage among hillbillies, as in: "Set a spell." **SETTIN**–*pres. tense.* Sitting. Billy Bob is likely to say: "Ah wuz jes a settin' 'round the haywz."

SHAAR *n.* Shower. A heavy rain or a method of bathing under a steady stream of water. Also *v.* The process of showering. "Ahma

151

gwine ta tike me a shaar."

SHAARD –*past tense*. This is mostly a Southern pronunciation and not partaken in too often by many hillbillies.

SHEE-OT *n.* Shit. This widely used pronunciation of this colorful word is generally reserved for use as an expression of disbelief or disgust and stands alone. For example, when Clem tells Lee Bob that his car is faster, Lee Bob will simply blurt out: "Shee-ot."

SHINDIG *n.* A party. This is another widely used expression among hillbillies, which indicates a party of any size, but is most often an informal affair and not usually a large celebration, like a "hootenany" or a "hoedown."

SHIVVY *n.* Chevy. A vehicle manufactured by the Chevrolet division of the General Motors Corporation. This is one of three types of vehicles that hillbillies recognize, the others being Fords and Dodges. Any other General Motors product, like a Buick, Oldsmobile or Pontiac are often referred to as "Shivvies" as well. Likewise Mercuries are Fords and Chryslers or Plymouths are Dodges. Hillbillies will, however, make a distinction between "Shivvies" and Cadillacs or between Fords and Lincolns, as the latter are considered superior vehicles, which carry some measure of prestige. There are also Jeeps, which are the traditional CJ variety and not those damn boxy things that the Yuppies drive. Practically any other vehicle is simply referred to disdainfully as, "Wun O M fern jobs." "Shivvy" is the pronunciation used universally by hillbillies.

SHORE *adj.* SURE. This pronunciation is of Southern origins, but is now heard throughout all regions.

SHOWIZ *contraction* of sure and is. Sure is. This way of saying this originated in the South, but is now in wide usage, as in: "Showiz a hot day, innit?"

SHOWNUF *contraction* of sure and enough. Sure enough. Like "showiz", this is of Southern origin, but enjoys wide usage these days. Actually both of these most likely had roots in the merging of speech patterns common among the blacks of the old South, however, in modern times most blacks are far too educated and sophisticated to use these pronunciations and they are now mostly relegated to trailer park trash. The classic example is: "Shownuff iz a wunner."

SHUCK *v.* Shirk. **SHUCKIN**. *–intr.* **SHUCHT** *–past tense* To rid oneself of something or to abandon something. In the case of hillbillies this is usually in reference to responsibility or duty, which is readily shirked by hillbillies everywhere. Maw might say: "Thet baw is shuckin his sponsibilities agin."

SICK HAIDIKE *n.* Sick headache. This is not a very common usage, but is heard among the traditional hillbillies of Appalachia and the

155

Southeast. I have heard it just a few times, but find it charming. It indicates the sort of headache that one gets from incessant annoyances. I once had a hair stylist in Myrtle Beach, S.C. tell me: "Ah wuz married wunst n' Lordy Ah luvd thet man, but he'd jes gimme a sick haidike."

SITCHYAYSHUN *n.* Situation. A combination of circumstances, a placement or position. This widely used pronunciation is an example of how hillbillies can jumble a word. "It's a bad sitchyayshhun."

SKAT *v.* A command to go away or to move along. This is usually directed at a child or animal as a means of sending it along its way. It is commonly shouted and

accompanied by an outward
sweeping hand gesture.

SKEERT *–past tense* of *v.* to scare.
Scared. Another example of the
"t" sound used to denote an "ed"
at the end of a word. This is in
wide use and is sometimes
prefixed with an a, thus becoming
ASKEERT. "Wots a matter, ya
askeert?"

SKIBBIES *n.* Slang for men's
underpants or briefs. Skivies.
This is a widespread hillbilly
classic, as in: "He were caught a
runnin thru the yard in is
skibbies."

SKOWEET *contraction* of let's go
eat. A great example of
economizing on verbage, this is
heard very commonly and not just
by hillbillies. At noon on

construction job-sites one will often hear someone say to their co-workers: "Skoweet."

SMAICK *v.* to strike with some force, usually suddenly with the hand. This can be either a slap or a punch and usually indicates a blow to the face. **SMAICKT** *–past tense* "He dun made me mad, soze Ah smaickt im." Most common in the South but heard regularly elsewhere.

SMAISH *v.* Smash. Another primarily Southern, but common usage in other regions. This can either mean to pulverize something or to punch specifically in the mouth. **SMAISHT**-*past tense* Smashed. A common example is: "Smaisht Taiters," which is a variation on "maisht taiters."

SMOKES *n.* Cigarettes. Nearly all hillbillies are voracious smokers. After all, their favorite pastime, NASCAR racing is heavily sponsored by Big Tobacco and besides, if it weren't for cigarette coupons, they wouldn't have any T-shirts to wear. At least once a day, your average hillbilly will say: "Ahma goan overta the store ta grap me sum smokes."

SNATCHT *past tense* of *v.* to snatch. Snatched. Once again we see the "t" sound replacing "ed" This is a variation on "grapt". A favorite hillbilly expression, especially among women who are fighting is: "Snatcht er bald." Common in all regions.

SOADYPOP *n.* a beverage consisting of carbonated water, sugar or artificial sweetener and

159

SMOKES

flavoring. This is almost exclusively a Northcentral usage, also sometimes just called **POP.** This is in contrast to the Southern usage of "Cocola." In the Northeast they refer to it as either "tonic" or simply as "soda".

SOD *n.* Side. This is primarily a Southern pronunciation, which has the same meaning as in plain English.

SOHN *n.* Sign. This is also a Southern pronunciation, having all the usual meanings, but is largely used among hillbillies to denote traces left behind by game animals, as in: "Deer sohn."

SOP *v.* Meaning to soak up. This is a hillbilly favorite everywhere, which can mean to soak up any liquid, like water or spills, but which often is used to denote soaking up gravy with some sort of bread or biscuit. Truck stop waitresses will say: "Hey thar hun, yawl want some biskits fer ta sop up thet thar grivey?"

SOT *n.* Sight. Mostly a Southern pronunciation, the noun form indicates something that is viewed, either pleasant, as in: "Hain't thet a loverly sot?" or hideous, as in "Wayall, ain't yew a sot." Also *adv.* Far. Used to denote a distance, as in: "a far sot." **SOTTIN'** *v. –tr* As in: "Ahma sottin in maw shotgun."

SOU' KACKLACKEY *place* South Carolina. This is a US state along the Atlantic Coast. This is a regional pronunciation, which is generally only heard in the

Carolinas. See also **NORT KACKLACKEY**

SOZE *adv.* So. This regularly heard hillbillyism is a favorite among hillbillies everywhere. It is generally only used, as an adverb, in mid-sentence, as in: "Ah ain't a goan, soze ya kin jes fergit it."

SPAR *v.* Spare. To refrain from causing harm or using. To save, be frugal, lenient or merciful. An example of this usage is: "Ah'll spar ya the embarrassment O tellein Paw wot ya dun." — *adj.* Extra or excess, as in: "Kin yawl spar some licker?" Another prime example is: "Spar tar," for spare tire. Both usages are primarily southern pronunciations, which are also heard occasionally elsewhere.

163

SPAWL *v.* Spoil. **SPAWLT** *–past tense* This is a primarily Southern pronunciation, as in: "Spar the rod, spawl the chile." In the past tense: "Thet baw shore is spawlt."

SPLAIN *v.* Explain. To make understood or to clarify a fact or subject. This is a fairly obscure pronunciation among hillbillies, being actually more common among Spanish speaking persons attempting this word in English, ala Rickie Ricardo, but in some contexts this pronunciation is used by hillbillies. The most common time it would be used is when it is in mid-sentence or following a word that ends in a vowel sound, as in: "Could yew splain it to me?" See also the more common pronunciation, **ESPLAIN.**

SPOASIN *v.* Suppose. While it would seem that this is a literal translation of the word "supposing," it is actually used in place of "suppose." This is usually stated by the hillbilly as conjecture, as in "Spoasin Ah doan wanna dew it?"

SPONSIBILITY *n.* Responsibility. This is something that hillbillies don't take too seriously. This one is widely heard, as in, "Yew gotsta tike sum sponsibility sooner er lyter."

SPONSIBUL *adj.* Responsible. This is also widely used and is merely the adjective form of the previous entry.

SPORT *v.* Support. This is another of those examples of hillbilly verbal economy and the penchant for running syllable together. A community minded hillbilly will "sport local sports."

STANNERT *n.* or *adj.* Standard. This word has many meanings, as in a stand or base, a measure of value or a degree of quality. This is the commonly used hillbilly pronunciation everywhere that hillbillies are found.

STAR *v.* Stare. Mostly an Ozark and Appalachian regional pronunciation, this one is also heard uttered by hard core hillbillies elsewhere, as in: "Stop n star."

STOLT *past tense* of *v.* to steal. Stolen. Another usage of the "t" sound, this is quite a common hillbilly word, as in: "He dun stolt im a core."

STOMPT *past tense* of *v.* to stomp. Stomped. This very common usage almost always means beat up, as in a fight. Billy Joe Jim Bob might proudly proclaim: "Wayull, Ah shore stompt thet sumbitch."

STRAVAGINT *adj.* Extravagant. Another wide usage and example of verbal hillbilly economy. Paw might say: "Attaire Country Buffette shore is stravagint."

STRENTH *n.* Strength. State or property of being strong, powerful, muscular intense or firm. This is a widely used pronunciation and it is not entirely clear why the "g" does not get pronounced, since this does not result in any real verbal economy, but this is the way the hillbillies pronounce it.

STRINEJER *n*. Stranger. One who is unfamiliar or unkown. This is largely a Southern pronunciation, as in: "Howdy Strinejer."

SUCCESSABLE *adj*. Susceptible. Readily subject to influence or force or just generally subject to. This is yet another glaring example of the jumbling of a complex word in the mind and mouth of the hillbilly. Heard among hard core hillbillies everywhere.

SUM *adj*. Some. Yes, I know that there is actually an English word; "sum", but that isn't how the hillbillies use it. As a matter of fact, this pronunciation is actually the accepted, and really the only one, used in the entire English speaking world, but it is worthy of noting that this spelling is actually the way it is said.

SUMBITCH *n.* Son of a bitch. This is a classic hillbilly pronunciation of a word that they just love to use with great frequency, not only to refer to someone for whom they have disdain, but also standing alone, as an expression of disgust or displeasure. This particular widely used hillbillyism was made extremely popular in the late 1970s by Jackie Gleason, in his role as Sheriff Buford T. Justice, in the "Smokey and The Bandit" movies.

SUMPIN' *pron.* Something. An unspecified or special thing. Another economical word usage, which is heard all over, even among many people who would not, strictly speaking, be considered hillbillies. Some classic hillbilly examples are: "Wayull, ain't thet sumpin'" or "Doan she thank she's sumpin'."

SUMPNUTHER *contraction* Something or other. This is another fine example of verbal economy in the hillbilly language, as in: "It's allways sumpnuther."

SUPPEENY *n.* Subpoena. A legal writ compelling an appearance in court or some tribunal. **SUPPEENEED** *–tr. v.* This is the exclusive hillbilly pronunciation of this word, but their spelling of it, if they can write at all, is all over the place. When they get one, hillbillies usually ignore it and are thus charged with contempt of court. Jimmy Joe might well complain: "Ah done got suppeeneed an iffn Ah doan show up, theyz a gwine haul ma ayuss off ta jile agin."

SUPPOSABLY *mod.* Supposedly. An indication of some presumption, as in: "Supposably, theyz goan ta haul Paw off ta jile fer not follerin' thet thar suppeeny." Another classic fumbling of a fairly simple word. This is another example of a pronunciation that is practically exclusive to hillbillies and is even heard way too often among those who should clearly know better.

SWANG *n.* Swing. An amusement item for children, which in the hillbilly world consists of a tire, hung from a tree limb by a rope. - *v.* to swing, as in swinging in the rope, swinging on the dance floor or engaging in sexual partner swapping or group sex.
SWANGIN', SWANGERS *–intr.*

SWUMP *n.* Swamp. A low lying piece of wetland.

SWUMPERS *n.* Waders. These are usually hip boots, but can sometimes also be chest waders. This is primarily a Northern usage, as in: "Weez a goan duck huntn, soze grap ya yer swumpers n tsko."

SYFERN *v.* To do mathematics or to calculate numbers. Probably deriving from the root word "decipher," this word has developed its own meaning in hillbillydom. This can also mean to do deep thinking on any topic in general, as in: "Ah been doin' me sum syfern an ta way ah gots er figgert . . ."

T

TA *prep.* To. This pronunciation would appear to have its origins in the farm country of the North and Midwest, but is currently in widespread usage. This word is often combined with and run together with other words to express various actions such as: "inta, upta, overta and daywnta." Also -*prep.* At. An example of this latter usage is: "Its ta the shop." This pronunciation is also sometimes used for the word "the".

TAIN'T *contraction* of it and ain't. I know that in proper English it should be "it is not," but remember how hillbillies feel about "M grammagical rules" and, after all, "Tain't no thang." This is a universal hillbilly usage.

TAITERS *n. –plur.* Potatoes. Originating in the South and probably stemming from Southern Blacks' usage, this has come to be a widespread usage. "Ya know, up Nawth, they doan eat no greeyats, they eats haish bronze with they aigs n baikin."

TALL *Contraction* of at and all. At all. An absolutely fabulous example of verbal economy, which is used very commonly, as in: "It doan matter tall."

TAR *n.* Tire. This is an item that sometimes goes on a car, but more often just sits in the yard or hangs by a rope from a tree, as a swing, to amuse "the yungunz."

Of course there are always several cars in the average hillbilly yard, however most of them have no tires attached thereto and sit on cement blocks with parts missing and the hood and trunk opened or missing. This is primarily a Southern pronunciation.

TAR ARN *n.* Tire iron. These are the tools that double as a car jack handles and a wrenches for removing lug nuts from car wheels, but among hillbillies they are also very popular as weapons. If you anger a hillbilly, look out, he's liable to "grap im a tar arn an give ya a whuppin upside the haid." This is mostly a Southern pronunciation.

TARNASHUN *n.* The best I can figure this is some sort of a place, like hell. Hillbillies use this word

TAR

TAR ARN

quite commonly in all regions, as in: "Wot in tarnashun R yew upta."

TARNFEATHER *v.* and *contraction* of tar and feather. This is an old hillbilly expression, but is not used much in actual practice anymore. In the old days, however, this was a fairly common way to punish someone for transgressions against ones family or the community in general. It involved actually covering an individual with hot tar, after they had been stripped naked, then covering them with feathers, while the tar was still hot, then running them off ones land or out of the town or the county. This barbaric ritual was invoked for a variety of reasons, such as stealing, getting caught having sex with ones child or wife or simply for being of the wrong race or ethnicity. The large decline in the use of this method is probably a blessing, however, in the case of some of today's arrogant criminals, it might be an efficient deterrent.

TAWK *v.* or *n.* to talk or talk. The act of speaking or the speech itself. *–past tense* **TAWKT**. *–pres tense* **TAWKIN**.

TAYUWOT *Phrase* Tell you what. This is a widely used hillbilly classic, used as an expression of appreciation, strong impression or disbelief. It is only very occasionally used in conjunction with other words, but is most commonly used all by itself and those surrounding the speaker almost always will understand its

179

meaning, in spite of the fact that
it can be used in a wide variety of
circumstances. A classic example
is when two or more hillbilly men
are out in public and see a highly
attractive female, one of them
will gesture and nudge another
and say with a nod, simply:
"Tayuwot!" They all will instantly
understand what it is that the
speaker is telling them.

TAYWN *n.* Town. Another primarily
Southern pronunciation, this must
be uttered in a single syllable.
This can be combined with either
"up" or "Daywn" to indicate
where one is going.

TEECHT *past tense* of *v.* to teach.
Taught. Kind of ironic, isn't it.
An example is: "Ah teecht thet
sumbitch ta be messin' wit me."
Widely used and say no more.

THANKIN *pres. tense* of *v.* to think. Thinking. Another piece of bittersweet irony. This is of Southern origin, but enjoys very wide usage.

THAR *adv.* There. Indicating some location, place or point in time, but also used as an introductory expletive. An example of the former usage is: "Thet one, thar," while an example the latter usage is: "Thar wunst wuz a gul . . ."

THEMTHAR *contraction* of them and there. Of course, in proper English this is actually "those there", but again we see the hillbillies' utter disregard for proper grammar and word usage. This one is heard all over, as in: "Themthar R the ownyus wuns they iz."

THET *adj.* That. This is the most common hillbilly pronunciation of that, which is heard in all regions. See also **HAT**

THETAWAY *contraction* of that and way. That way. This is primarily a Midwestern, Western and Ozark usage, but is not uncommon in other localities. The classic example is: "They went thetaway."

THEYZ *possessive* form of the third person *pron.* they or *contraction* of they and are. Theirs or they are. This is widely heard and an example the former usage is: "Its theyz," while a classic example of the latter is: "Theyz goan uptaywn."

THISSEAR *contraction* of this and here. This here. Indicates a specific thing, which is present while being referred to. Another widely heard usage, as in: "Thissear iz the bestest wun they iz."

THROWED *past tense* of *v.* to throw. Thrown. This is virtually the only usage that hillbillies make of the past tense reference of this verb, as in: "Ah wuz throwed fer a loop." Notice, however, that this utilizes the "ed" sound and not the "t" sound, unlike so many other hillbillyisms.

THUMPT *past tense* of *v.* to thump. This is widely used, but generally has a fairly narrow meaning. It usually means to rap on something with ones knuckles, as in: "He thumpt on the table" or to bump into something, usually with the

183

head, as in: "Ah thumpt ma haid on the core door." It can, however, also be used to indicate bumping with other than the head, but this usage is not as commonly heard.

THUNK *past tense* of *v.* to think. Thought. Another wide usage with trailer park types, wherever they can be found. This is a result of hillbilly logic that tells them that if its: "stink, stank, stunk" and "drink, drank, drunk," it must therefore be "think, thank, thunk." Frighteningly enough, this actually makes some sense.

TIKE *v.* To take. This originated in the South, but has spread like wildfire elsewhere, as in "Tike me out ta the ballgame." **TUCK**. – *past tense*. Took. This pronunciation is also the preferred one for hillbillies everywhere, as in: "Ah dun tuck thet baw out ahind the woodshed an give im a whuppin'."

TIN *n.* Ten. While Southern in origin, this one has become the standard hillbilly pronunciation of the number ten everywhere.

TOLT *past tense* of *v.* to tell. Told. Again we see the "d" sound in English liberally replaced by the "t" sound in hillbillyese. This is heard far and wide, as in: "Hiffn I tolt ya wunst, Ah tolt ya a hunnert toms."

TOM *n.* Time. Mostly a Southern pronunciation, it is also said this way by non-hillbilly Southerners, as in "Tom morches own."

TOMMORRY *n.* Tomorrow. The day after today. This is a far flung usage among hard core hillbillies, as in: "It kin wait til tommorry."

TRANNY *n.* Transmission. As in the power transmission assembly in an automobile, including the shifting mechanism and the gear box. This is virtually the only way that a hillbilly will ever refer to this mechanism. Hillbillies are very often working on their "tranny."

TROTH *n.* Trough. Any kind of assemblage, which forms a valley for holding substances, usually liquids or livestock feed. Paw will order his son: "Baw, go out n slop em hawgs n fill M troths up good."

TSKO *contraction* of let us go. Let's go. This is a wonderful shortening of an entire expression into four letters and does wonders for verbal economy. This one is actually enjoyed quite widely, even beyond the hillbilly community.

TUCK *past tense* of *v.* to take. Taken or took. This is the highly preferred hillbilly usage of either of these words, as in: "Ah tuck the core upta the shop ta work on the tranny."

TURREL *n.* Towel. This pronunciation is common in the hill country of the Southeast and the Ozarks and, interestingly enough is also the pronunciation in some boroughs of New York and New Jersey. This is a fairly obscure usage in modern times, but is still heard occasionally back in the hills.

TWO-TRACKIN' *v.* This is an activity which is extremely popular in rural, wooded areas throughout the USA, which involves driving wildly, usually in a "forbuhfor" along trails through the woods, swamps and brush, which are generally no more than double wheel ruts, ergo; "two-trackin'." This activity is enjoyed primarily by teenagers, but is also widely partaken in by mental juveniles of all ages, which is a hillbilly man of any age.

U

UNCA *n.* Uncle. This is how hillbillies everywhere refer to a brother of their parent or grandparent. The "kits" might say: "Oh baw, weez a goan ta Unca Clems haywz."

UPTA *contraction* of up and to. Up to. Usually a reference to some place, as in; "Weeuz upta unca Dayal haywz." This is primarily a Northern, Midwestern and Western usage. Also denotes one engaging in some activity, as in: "thet baw's upta sumpnuther."

UPTOWN *n.* This is the Northern pronunciation, whereas in the South its pronounced **UPTAYWN** in two syllables. This probably originated among the settlers in

189

farm country, because the farms were generally situate on the low ground, or "bottomlands" and the towns were built on hills or high ground, so that when one went to town one would ascend in altitude to get "uptown."

USNZ *pron.* Us *first person plural objective.* This usage is fairly common, but only among pretty hard core hillbillies. It is used in most instances where proper English would call for simply the use of "us", as in: "It's jes usnz."

V

VAYLANSE *n.* Valance. A short hanging drape along the top of a window, ledge or canopy. This is the hillbilly pronunciation, especially in the South and West. Also widely used by hillbillies to describe the air damn on an automobile, particularly a "NAYZCORE ricin core."

VETINARYUN *n.* Veterinarian. An animal doctor.

VIDDELS *n.* Food for human consumption of any variety.

VON *n.* Vine. This is where grapes grow and are also varieties of ivy. You know the old song: "Bottle of won, fruit of the von."

191

W

WANNA *contraction* of want and to. Want to. This is extremely common and is heard not only among hillbillies, but is actually the American standard pronunciation.

WAWK *v.* to walk. **WAWKT, WAWKIN'** *intr.* This is almost exclusively a Southern pronunciation, as in: "Ah wawkt ta the store."

WAWTCH *v.* to watch. Watch. To observe something. Of course, there have been many hillbillies whose last words were: "Hey yawl, Wawtch this." Also *n.* A small timekeeping device, either worn on the wrist or carried in a pocket.

WAWTER *n.* Water. This is the Southern pronunciation, while in the extreme Northern regions of the Mid states and Canada it is pronounced **WAHTER.**

WAYULL *adj. or adv.* Well. Meaning satisfactory, good or proper or in good health. *-n.* As in a source of liquid or gas from the ground, as in: "wawter wayull." This is largely a Southern pronunciation.

WEEUZ *contraction* of we was, which in English is, of course, we *were*, but remember the rule about hillbillies and grammar: ie; there are none. This is a wide usage, as in: "Weeuz headin ta taywn yesterdee."

WEEZ *contraction* of we and is. We is. Don't give me that grammar crap. I know it should be "are", but this is a hillbilly dictionary and hillbillies "don't give no damn 'bout no grammar." Another combining of words, albeit not much economy. This is widely heard, as in: "Weez a goan ta the store."

WEUNZ *pron.* We *first person plural proper*. This is similar to **USNZ**, but is used as we in sentences, as in: "Weeunz is goan ta Maw's haywz." See also **USNZ**.

WHAR *adv.* Where. This is an inquisitive form of placement, situation or position, as in: "Whar R yew?" -*conj.* Of placement or situation, as in: "The big city iz whar the action iz." Also *n.* a location, as in: "Its uptaywn, thet's whar."

WHEELBARREL *n.* Wheelbarrow. This is a hand- operated container on one or two wheels for hauling dirt, rocks, or other articles. Used primarily in lawn care and maintenance, this is the preferred pronunciation among hillbillies far and wide.

WHOLST *conj.* While or Whilst. This is the most common hillbilly usage of the conjecture form of While and is similar to the British usage of whilst. Obviously this one has its roots in the traditional hillbilly homelands of Great Britain. An example of its usage is: "Yew yungunz wait here wholst ah go inta the store."

195

WHOONT *contraction* of who would not. Who Wouldn't. This is another example of the hillbilly knack for running words together, as in: "Whoont wanna go ta the rices?"

WHUPPIN' *pres.* tense of *v.* to whup. To beat up. To brutalize. While this event sounds like it might involve a whip, it almost never does. It usually involves bare fists, chairs, rifle butts and the like. This word can be a verb as in; "Clem give thet boy got a whuppin' fer caitin' around wit iz wife"; or as a noun; "Baw, Weez agonna give yew a whuppin'."

WHUPT *past tense* of *v.* to whup. Brutalized. This is simply the past tense form of the preceding entry, as in: "Ah whupt thet baw good."

WHUPPIN'

WHUTFER *contraction* of what and for. What for. A scolding or tongue lashing. This is a common usage, as in to "give um whutfer." This can also be a question asked upon huving a command given or request made, as in: "Whutfer yew want me ta dew thet?"

WINDER *n.* Window. This is Southern in origin, but is now heard quite commonly elsewhere. "Baw, git up n close thet winder affore the whole fambly freezes."

WIT *prep.* With. To accompany, be a companion of or possess an attribute or characteristic. Also to be in support of or in concert with. In regard to or in comparison. This is a preferred hillbilly usage everywhere, as in: "Yew wanna come wit?"

WOE UP *v.* to slow. Slow down.
WODE UP *–past tense* This is
largely a Southern usage, which is
used very often by NASCAR TV
announcers. In fact this is the
only way that I have ever heard
them refer to the act of slowing
down, as in: "Thet olbaw best woe
up goan inta thet corner er he'll
git er all cattywompus."

WON *n.* Wine. A fermented fruit
drink, usually made from grapes,
but hillbillies also who drink it,
often make their own from
dandelions, strawberries, apples
or any other fruit or buy the
cheap apple or grape varieties.

WORSH *v.* To wash or clean. This
is a very wide usage and God only
knows where the R sound comes
from, but that's how they say it.
This one is heard very often and

WORSHIN' YER SKIBBIES

in most all regions of the
continent.

WORSHINGTON *n.* This can be the
State, the First President of the
USA or anyone else with the same
surname, but usually it is in
reference to the Nation's Capital,
WORSHINGTON D.C., or as
some hardcore hillbillies still
refer to it: **WORSHINGTON
CITY**. This pronunciation is
widely heard.

WOT *pron.* What. Which thing. An
interrogatory identification. This
is another widely heard
pronunciation, as in: "Wot yew
tawkin bout, baw?"

WOWK *v.* Walk. This is
predominantly a Southern
pronunciation, while in the North
they prefer **WAHK.**

WUNNER *n.* or *v.* Wonder. *–intr.* **WUNNERIN', WUNNERT, WUNNERZ** This can either be a noun for astonishment, puzzlement or doubt or a verb, as in to be curios about or inquisitive. This has Southern origins, but has become quite common throughout the hillbilly world, as in: "Ahza wunnerin' wot yewza thanking."

WUNST *adv.* Once. One time only or finally, as in: "Wunst n fer all." *-n.* As in a single occurrence suddenly or all at one time, as in: "All ta wunst." This is an extremely common hillbilly usage.

WUNT *contraction* of would and not. Wouldn't. Also sometimes pronounces **WOONT**. This is quite a common usage. As in: "Ah wunt dew it iffn Ah wur yew."

WUR *plur second person singular past indicative* of *v.* to be. Were. An example of this usage is: "Whar wur yew?" More commonly, however, *first* and *third person singular past indicative* of *v.* to be. Was. This grossly improper usage is the more widely used among hillbillies, as in: "Ah wur daywn ta the pork." Occasionally hillbillies will use **WUZ** for "was," but more commonly misuse it as "were." Go figure.

WURD *n.* Word. Well once again, I confess that this is actually the common pronunciation among nearly all Americans, but, as this one does differ a bit from the pronunciation of the true King's English, it is worthy of note herein.

WUZ *plur second person singular past indicative* of *v.* to be. Were. While this is actually the common American pronunciation of *the first person singular past indicative:* "was," it is not usually used by hillbillies in the proper sense, but is more widely misused as in: "They wuz careynon, soze Ah thumpt M in the haid."

Y

Y *adv.* or *interj.* Why. For what purpose. This is the pronunciation used everywhere by hillbillies and even quite commonly by those who are not, strictly speaking, hillbillies at all. Examples of this abound anytime the word "why" is used.

YAHOO! *Interj.* A cheer or yell of joy, which must be bellowed at the top of ones lungs. This is the Western version of this cheer most commonly used in Texas and surrounding states. Also *n.* Meaning an oafish person or buffoon, but this usage of the word is not really common among hillbillies, but is reserved for the

"Hoypolloy." See also **YEEE HAWWWW!!!!**

YAWL *contraction* of you and all. You all. This is a reference to the second person plural. This is primarily Southern and has become cliché, so now has come into common usage elsewhere. See also **YOOUNZ**.

YEEE HAWWWW!!!! *Interj.* Like **YAHOO!** this is an exclamation of great joy, but is the more Southeastern version. This word does not have the Noun usage.

YER *poss.* form of *pron.* you. Your. A very common usage, as in: "Its yer life, dew as yew please." This is also a IcontractionI of you and are, as in: "yer gawna git a whuppin now baw."

YERSEFF *pron.* This is the special usage of the second person, which much like "yer," is in common usage, as in: "Dew it yerseff."

YESTERDEE *n.* Yesterday. The day before today. This is the pronunciation of choice among hillbillies. The "ay" sound is replaced by an "ee" sound. This is also the case with the days of the week. These are: **SUNDEE, MUNDEE, TEWZDEE, WENZDEE, THURZDEE, FRYDEE** and **SATTERDEE**.

YEW *pron.* You. The second person singular or plural. This is widely used and is in fact the standard English pronunciation pretty much everywhere.

YEWZA *pron.* You or you are. This pronunciation is very much a

hillbilly usage in all regions. Its
use is, for the most part, limited
to situations where an intention or
action is indicated for the second
person, usually limited to the
singular, as in: "Yewza gawna
gitcherseff in trouble, baw."
When used in the second person
plural **YAWL** or **YAWLZA** is the
preferred usage, but this latter
usage is much more obscure.

YONNER *adj.* or *adv.* Yonder.
Being at an indicated distance or
place. This is almost exclusively
a Southern pronunciation, as in:
"Lookie over yonner."

YOOUNZ *pron. plural second
person* You. This usage, which is
mostly heard in the South and
Midwest, is an indication that the
second persons being referenced
are not singular, but plural, as in:

"Yoounz kin come wit iffn ya wanna." See also **YAWL.**

YUNGUNZ *n.* Children or young people. Literally translated I suppose this would be "young ones." This is how hillbillies refer to any collection of young persons of wide age range, as in: "Gather the yungunz round." If only small children are being referred to, the preferred usage is **KITS.**

<u>Z</u>

ZACKTLY *adv.* Exactly. In an accurate, precise or exact manner. This is a widely used pronunciation among hillbillies, as in: "Yawl dew zacktly as yew please."

ZADGERATE *v.* Exaggerate. **ZADGERATUT, ZADGERATIN'** —*tr.* To magnify or make greater than is actually the truth. To enlarge or increase disproportionately, overstate or enlarge unrealistically.

ABOUT THE AUTHOR

Tomhorn Legghorn is really Thomas C. Legg, JD, Lawyer, Land Developer, Lumber Dealer, Farmer and Hillbilly Author. He was born the youngest of two privileged sons of highly educated and intelligent people, Louis E. "Ned" and Joan M. Legg on September 9, 1956 in Lansing, Michigan, roughly two years after Louis III, who is by far the more sophisticated, bright and socially acceptable son. He was raised in Okemos, Michigan and Graduated from The Dublin School in Dublin, N.H. in 1974, where he was sent by the family, so that the neighbors would stop talking about that "problem child at the Legg house." After attending a series of colleges and universities on the "7 year plan", he finally graduated (Barely) from Kansas Newman College in Wichita, Kansas in June of 1981 (It is still widely believed that he was only graduated because the nuns couldn't tolerate him any longer). After several years wasted as a ski bum in the Rockies, his benevolent brother and father roped him into the family lumber business, where he spent a few years as a store manager, followed by 10 years as comptroller (in the back office, where he wouldn't keep pissing off the customers). As a mid-life crisis, instead of taking up with a younger women, Tom went to Law School at The Thomas M. Cooley Law School in Lansing, Michigan, from which he graduated in April 1997 in that 5% of his class that made the top 95% possible. He miraculously passed the Michigan Bar Exam in July of 1997 and practices law in Coldwater, Michigan, where he lives and also is still involved in the family business, until his brother or father catch him and pay him to leave. He lives with his fiance' (They're probably married by now) Kristin Corlett and some cats. He flies seaplanes, hunts, fishes, skis and does other outdoorsy stuff for fun. He fancies himself as the Crowned Prince of the Hillbillies, much to his dear mother's dismay.